THE LANGUAGE LABORATORY
AND
MODERN LANGUAGE TEACHING

THE LANGUAGE LABORATORY

AND

MODERN LANGUAGE TEACHING

EDWARD M. STACK

New York · OXFORD UNIVERSITY PRESS · *1960*

THIS BOOK is designed to assist language teachers and students in training to become language teachers. It provides specific descriptions of techniques and procedures for the classroom, language laboratory, and collateral activities. Particular attention is given to the beginning and intermediate stages of instruction. The aural-oral approach, combined with the best features of the "traditional" approach, is the guiding philosophy of the presentation. Practical guidance, rather than philosophical argumentation, is the aim of this text.

The optimum sequence of presentation of a language is recommended by a committee of the Modern Language Association, and that sequence is scrupulously followed throughout. The sequence is HEARING–SPEAKING–READING–WRITING on the high school and university level; it is reduced to HEAR–SAY–SEE in elementary school language programs, known as FLES (Foreign Language in the Elementary School).

High school and university programs for the teaching of beginning and intermediate language do not differ appreciably; the introduction of the language is basically the same from the teacher's point of view. However, the earlier a student begins his language study, the better off he will be. Any slight differences in techniques are noted as each subject is discussed in this book, but generally the same procedures apply to all age groups. Elementary school programs, too, will be able to adapt the same procedures, except that all reading and writing will be deferred and vocabulary will be kept very concrete and simple.

Notice that there are problems and exercises for each chapter. These are grouped together at the end of the book. Students preparing for a teaching career, as well as teachers learning laboratory techniques, will profit by applying their ingenuity and imagination to solving the practical problems posed.

This text includes both teaching techniques and administrative and mechanical techniques relating to the operation of a language laboratory. Since the recent development of special language-teaching machinery, the teacher must be prepared to administer the functioning of a laboratory. Only thus can full advantage be taken of the advances that have been made in the realm of audio-visual aids specifically designed for language teaching.

Intentionally excluded from this text are descriptions and operational data on particular brands of machinery—tape recorders, projectors, and the like—because each machine is best mastered by actual practice. The multiplicity of types of equipment is such as to forbid examination of each kind in this textbook. Instead, the general functions that can be carried out by any of the equipment are organized and studied.

I wish to thank the following persons for their assistance: Mr. Leo Baugus and Mr. George Grasty, my colleagues at Whittier College, and Mr. Igor Budzinsky.

Teachers and students using this book are invited to send the author contributions of new techniques, criticisms, and other comments for use in future editions. Please send these to Villanova University, Modern Language Department, Villanova, Pennsylvania.

EDWARD M. STACK

Whittier, California
March 1960

Contents

THE LANGUAGE LABORATORY

AND

MODERN LANGUAGE TEACHING

I

The Force of Language

THE FUNCTION of language is to communicate ideas. When we speak the same language as someone else, that common language is a force for unity and sympathy on every level—from individuals and families to national and ethnic groups. When two businessmen are able to agree readily and completely, we hear one of them say of the other, "Jones talks my language." We are, on the other hand, suspicious, fearful, and hostile when confronted with strangers speaking an unknown language. When surrounded by hundreds of people speaking, let us say, Bantu, we would greet with enthusiasm another English speaker—though we may have little else in common with him. The inability to communicate can be a frightening thing, and until we are placed in a situation where we cannot make our thoughts and wishes known because of a difference in language, we do not realize how much we value this ability.

Even within a language there are social and dialectical differences that arouse fear and distrust. It is a universal human trait to shun the unusual and unfamiliar. It is easy to imagine that the problem is magnified greatly when a totally different language (rather than merely a social or regional dialect of the *same* language) is involved.

Language and culture are inextricably woven together, and a comprehension of one without the other is impossible. The logic of one language is not necessarily that of another, yet both may lead to the same conclusion. The American student who learns that a week in French is referred to as *huit jours* (eight days) thinks that the calendar must have been overhauled, until he learns that the French count from Monday to Monday and *include the day on which the count starts*. Or again, the method of numbering the floors of a building is a part of the culture and logic inherent in the language, and a translation of *troisième étage* as "third floor" would lead to wasted time, unless the hearer knew that this was the fourth floor under the United States system. It would likewise seem

3

most ridiculous for a little French boy to shout, "Hurrah! It's Thursday!" unless the hearer knew that Thursday is a school holiday in France, and that this exclamation is the equivalent of the American boy's "Hurrah! It's Saturday!" These are examples of the culture in its manifestation through language, and without the one, the understanding of the other cannot exist.

Language and culture should be taught together. Through this instruction we gain tolerance and understanding of another point of view, another system of logical reasoning, and another texture of civilization. Even where this insight does not lead to acceptance or agreement, at least it gives us the knowledge necessary for an understanding of the other culture and its members.

Objectives of Modern Language Teaching. The objective which may be set for language teaching is to enable students to understand, speak, read, and write the foreign language with native speed; intonation, pronunciation, accent, and fluency of speech should be that of an educated native speaker in normal conversation. This objective is difficult to realize fully. There must be good co-operation of students, parents, and educators, good motivation, and a reasonable degree of native ability on the part of the students. When these conditions exist we can achieve considerable success if:

1. Language study is begun at an early age.
2. Instruction has continuity over a period of years.
3. The student is brought as completely as possible into contact with the language.
4. Structural linguistic methods are used to systematize language patterns and speech, thus shortening the learning process and reducing the haphazard mode of learning characteristic of the way in which one's native language is learned (over a period of time).

The best time for a child to start learning a second language is in elementary school; deferring this study to high school or even college is undesirable. Likewise, a break in instruction—omitting study of the language, once started—of an academic year or even of a semester, will seriously set back the progress of a young student. Lessons must be systematically pursued, and parental encouragement and assistance should be enlisted.

The FLES (Foreign Language in the Elementary School) program of the Modern Language Association is the first organized step in the direction of starting children early in the language learning process. The interest of the PTA and the co-operation of educational administrators have enabled language teachers in many communities to set up very successful programs for elementary school children. Los Angeles and San Diego, among many other cities, have extensive FLES programs; many universities, such as Stanford University and the University of California, have conducted FLES workshops for the special training of language teachers of elementary school children.

Teaching Order of Procedure. The order in which the language skills are presented is that recommended by the Textbook Committee of the Modern Language Association. The order on the high school and university level is HEARING–SPEAKING–READING–WRITING. This means that a student first hears a word, phrase, or sentence (perhaps accompanied by a visual aid for showing meaning), then imitates what he has heard. When he has become proficient in recognizing and reproducing the sounds, he learns to read and write. This technique makes the student concentrate on the essential feature of language—*sound*—and eliminates reliance on printed words until mastery of sound is achieved.

Reading and writing may lag only a lesson or two behind the aural-oral presentation. It is a matter of judging when the students have thoroughly learned to hear and say a word, so that their pronunciation will not be adversely affected by their seeing the word in print. In French, for example, the spelling of the word for "cat" (*le chat*) is not given and tested by dictation until the teacher is sure that nobody will pronounce the word as it appears, using English values for the letters. After the point of sureness in hearing and speaking has been reached for this word, the teacher may require the last two steps of reading and writing it.

The procedure for FLES programs would be reduced to the steps HEAR–SAY–SEE, with writing omitted until about the second or third year of study.

Aural-Oral Drills. To meet the needs of the first two steps—hearing and speaking—pattern drills are used. These pattern drills present various features of the language in a systematic way for the beginner. They consist of a series of examples of a *single* grammatical or pronunciation feature that is new, but make use of material already learned as part of the phrases presented. Since a pattern is established, the student will soon be making his own statements following the established form. Pattern drills can be easily recorded and used in the language laboratory.

Some of the techniques for preparing aural-oral pattern drills will be covered in later chapters.

Classroom Procedures. Classroom instruction and language laboratory drills complement each other. The language laboratory relieves the teacher of endless repetition of patterns, and frees class time for flexible applications of the language. Many of the traditional methods are adaptable here, with the notable exception of the extensive use of English and of translation exercises, which are reduced to a minimum. The memorization of "rules" is eliminated for the most part.

Tests and Measurements. Techniques to test a student's comprehension of oral language, and of his ability to express himself immediately, accurately, and with native pronunciation, are quite different from those traditionally used to test written comprehension and composition. Yet traditional methods can be adapted for some of the aural-oral testing systems. Aural Comprehension Tests and Oral Examinations will form the subject matter of a separate chapter.

Language Laboratories. The most important advance in language teaching efficiency is the language laboratory. The teacher must know something about the physical requirements of a laboratory, how to operate it, how to orient and train students to use it, and what preparations must be made for class use of the laboratory. These are matters to be considered in three general chapters. Since there are two main types of laboratories—library and broadcast systems—they will be distinguished according to their functions, modes of operation, advantages and disadvantages. The library system is suitable for university students capable of independent study; the broadcast system is well adapted to high school and elementary school laboratories where a class works together under a teacher's direction.

Construction of Aural–Oral Drills

APPLICATION of the aural-oral method requires that the student's first contact with the foreign language be that of hearing and understanding; and that the second step be that of intelligent imitation of what he has heard, with careful attention to accent, rhythm, intonation, and pronunciation. Instructional drills need to be constructed in such a way that the student is freed from all reliance on printed materials, at least until he has a sure mastery of the sound production of a given unit of work. Language is a system of communication by *sound,* and written symbols are quite secondary to the oral system in courses for the beginner. Reading and writing objectives will be introduced gradually as each segment of work is mastered orally and aurally; these graphic skills will be more thoroughly learned and understood if they are based upon aural and oral proficiency in the language.

Drills (by which *aural-oral* drills is meant henceforth) consist principally of sense-making units of the foreign language, spoken with native speed and pronunciation. The utterances are grouped in *patterns;* that is, several examples of a single grammatical or phonetic feature are grouped together so that the student will hear the consistency and be able to apply the pattern to succeeding examples. Since these drills are spoken (and usually recorded on magnetic tape) in the foreign language, and since all responses on the part of the student are likewise in the foreign language, there can be no blanks to fill in, no English words in parentheses, devices so common in printed drills in textbooks. These and other similar devices have been a part of the teaching material for so long that it sometimes comes as a shock to teachers to discover that the drills in their textbook cannot be converted into oral drills merely by reading them onto a magnetic tape. It is very difficult to read a blank or a set of parentheses for a recording, and impossible for the student to make out what is expected of him.

English should be eliminated from the exercises. Encourage the student to associate his ideas directly in the foreign language rather than to go through the intermediary of his native tongue. Inclusion of translation exercises merely engrains the student's reliance on English. Frenchmen have been getting along very well in French for hundreds of years without recourse to English, and it should be pointed out to the student that the foreign language is a self-sufficient mode of communication which he can use effectively—and independently of English.

In selecting a textbook for use with the aural-oral approach, beware of those texts having many exercises containing blanks, words in parentheses, English translation, or other exercises stressing the written and English-oriented aspects. Many modern textbooks, even those purporting to be "conversational," are provided with a preponderance of such undesirable drills. If such a text is adopted, the teacher will need to be prepared to reorganize and recast the material (grammatical principles as well as vocabulary) into patterned drills that can be presented orally. Some existing textbooks contain many exercises of the following kinds, all unsuitable for oral drills:

Example 1: *Supply the appropriate verb form:*
　　　　　1. Nous (*will finish it*) _____ demain.
　　　　　2. Il (*will go there*) _____ samedi.

Example 2: *Supply the appropriate preposition:*
　　　　　1. Permettez-moi _____ continuer.
　　　　　2. Je tiens _____ partir.

Example 3: *Give the correct form of the verb indicated:*
　　　　　1. nosotros _____ (tener)
　　　　　2. yo _____ (ir)

Example 4: *Supply* ce, il, elle, elles, *or* ils:
　　　　　1. _____ est vrai.
　　　　　2. _____ est Anglais.
　　　　　3. _____ est très jolie.

Example 5: *Supply the correct form of the adjective:*
　　　　　1. Dort steht ein (*old*) Mann.
　　　　　2. Da kommt ein (*small*) Kind.
　　　　　3. Voilà une (*beautiful*) maison.
　　　　　4. Cette dame est (*charming*).

Example 6: *Translate into French (Spanish, German, etc.)*
　　　　　1. We are reading a good book.
　　　　　2. Our house is near the library.

Examples 1 and 5 would require the mixing of English and the foreign language in the same sentence, and this would result in a confusing and ludicrous recording. Examples 2 and 4 would require the speaker to omit words in the midst of a sentence, then continue as if nothing had happened. Example 6 is obviously suitable only as a written exercise. None of the examples shown show careful patterning: Example 1 has a regular verb followed by an irregular one, and a different kind of word is mixed with the verb in each case (*it* and *there*); In Example 2 the *de*-pattern started in the first sentence is not continued; Example 3 does not stay with the *nosotros* form, and it has two irregular verbs so that a pattern is impossible—and so on. The lack of pattern and the impossible form (from the oral point of view) make these exercises unusable as oral drills. Yet they were designed to elicit a specific response and to achieve a particular teaching objective.

Faced with such textbook exercises, the teacher may write a script for oral drills based on the grammatical content and vocabulary of each unit. Here are examples of ways of eliciting the same information and responses:

Example 1 is an attempt to teach (or perhaps only *test*) the future tense. It contains the error of calling for two things at once—a verb *and* a pronoun or adverb. First omitting the pronoun problem, which should be the subject of separate drills, the future tense could be elicited as follows:

> TAPE: Jean finira la leçon demain. Et nous?
> STUDENT: Nous **finirons** la leçon demain.

> TAPE: Jean choisira un bon livre. Et nous?
> STUDENT: Nous **choisirons** un bon livre.
>> (Six more regular **-ir** verbs in the **nous**-form are elicited before moving on to another person and to other types of verbs.)

> TAPE: Je vais à la plage samedi. Et Robert?
> STUDENT: Il **va** à la plage samedi.

Example 2 had the purpose of teaching the use of prepositions before infinitives. An oral drill might elicit the same responses by use of a fixed increment drill, in which the tape starts a sentence which the student finishes with a standard ending:

Complete each fragment with the phrase **étudier le français:**

TAPE: Permettez-moi . . .
STUDENT: Permettez-moi **d'étudier le français.**

TAPE: Alain cesse . . .
STUDENT: Alain cesse **d'étudier le français.**
(Six more examples requiring *de*)

TAPE: Georges continue . . .
STUDENT: Georges continue **à étudier le français.**

TAPE: Georges tient . . .
STUDENT: Georges tient **à étudier le français.**
(Six more examples requiring *à*)

TAPE: Alain aime . . .
STUDENT: Alain aime **étudier le français.**

TAPE: Georges veut . . .
STUDENT: Georges veut **étudier le français.** etc.

Example 3 could be recast into an oral drill to teach these irregular verbs, using the analogy drill. This drill gives a stimulus with the verb in use in a sense-making utterance, then asks for use of the same verb in another person:

Answer the inquiry:
TAPE: Ella tiene hambre. ¿Y usted?
STUDENT: **Yo tengo** hambre.

TAPE: Nosotros tenemos calor. ¿Y Carlos?
STUDENT: **Carlos tiene** calor.

TAPE: Pablo va a la iglesia. ¿Y usted?
STUDENT: **Yo voy** a la iglesia.

Example 4 is intended to teach the student to select *ce* or a regular subject pronoun as the subject of *est*. As it stands, it is merely a test in writing. This grammatical principle may be taught by the following pattern:

Combine the following short sentences into a single sentence, using **c'est un** *or* **c'est une:**

33. Voilà Gaston. Il est professeur.
    STUDENT: **C'est un** professeur.

34. Voilà Lucien. Il est ingénieur.
    STUDENT: **C'est un** ingénieur. etc.

Combine the pairs, using **il est** *or* **elle est:**

42. Voilà Gaston. C'est un Français.
    STUDENT: **Il est** Français.

47. Voilà Marie. C'est une parisienne.
    STUDENT: **Elle est** parisienne.

As for Example 5, adjectives can be elicited through oral drills without blanks and words in parentheses in the following manner:

Combine the following pairs into single sentences:

1. Dort steht ein Mann. Er ist alt.
   STUDENT: Dort steht **ein alter Mann.**

5. Dort steht eine Frau. Sie ist alt.
   STUDENT: Dort steht **eine alte Frau.**

54. Voilà une maison. Elle est belle.
    STUDENT: Voilà **une belle maison.**

67. Voilà un professeur. Il est bon.
    STUDENT: Voilà **un bon professeur.** etc.

These two sets of examples—those in the textbook as contrasted with those for oral drill—show that the same objectives can be attained without the use of blanks, inserted English, and other typographical devices. The remainder of this chapter will be a presentation of similar methods for the construction of oral drills. These methods will be listed by parts of speech or function. The general principles applying are as follows:

1. Teach only one new thing at a time.
2. Keep the utterances short.
3. Establish and hold a pattern for at least eight utterances.

The mechanical problems of drill construction relating to how many pairs of responses to use for teaching a given grammatical principle, the method of preparing and recording scripts, and the different arrangements of drills will be discussed in the next chapters. Here we are dealing

only with model *pairs* (stimulus-response pairs) that have specific usefulness in certain grammatical presentations.

1. Adjectives. The two main problems are the position and the agreement of adjectives. In French, agreement is presented by applying an
adjective to a feminine noun in the stimulus. The student responds by
applying the same adjective to a masculine noun, thus learning that the
principle is to omit the final consonant sound from the feminine to form
the masculine. The masculine noun is suggested in the stimulus:

*Apply the adjective used in the first half of each sentence to the
noun suggested in the second half.*

41. Cette jeune fille est **intelligente.** Et le garçon?
    STUDENT: Le garçon est **intelligent.**

42. Cette table est **intéressante.** Et le livre?
    STUDENT: Le livre est **intéressant.**

43. Cette maison est **grande.** Et le château?
    STUDENT: Le château est **grand.**

50. Cette maison est **blanche.** Et le mur?
    STUDENT: Le mur est **blanc.**

1. La pluma es **negra.** ¿Y el lápiz?
   STUDENT: El lápiz es **negro.**

2. La señora es **alta.** ¿Y el señor?
   STUDENT: El señor es **alto.**

3. Esta muchacha es **mexicana.** ¿Y este muchacho?
   STUDENT: Este muchacho es **mexicano.**

1. Стол коричневый. А кровать?
   STUDENT: Кровать (тоже) коричневая.[1]

9. Учитель умен. А учительница?
   STUDENT: Учительница (тоже) умна.[2]

17. Это интересная книга. А словарь?
    STUDENT: Словарь (тоже) интересный.[3]

[1] The table is brown. How about the bed?
The bed is (also) brown.
[2] The teacher (*m.*) is intelligent. How about the [lady] teacher?
The lady teacher is (also) intelligent.
[3] This book is interesting. And the dictionary?
The dictionary is (also) interesting.

Adjective position (preceding or following the noun) can be taught as follows:

> *Rephrase the following sentences, using* c'est un *or* c'est une *and incorporating the adjective in its correct position:*

83. Voilà un chat qui est **content**.
    STUDENT: C'est **un chat content**.

84. Voilà un élève qui est **riche**.
    STUDENT: C'est **un élève riche**.

. . .

90. Voilà une dame qui est **vieille**.
    STUDENT: C'est **une vieille dame**.

92. Je pense à la maison qui est **petite**.
    STUDENT: C'est **une petite maison**. etc.

Similarly in Spanish the following drill could be used:

11. El muchacho es **alto**.
    STUDENT: Es **un muchacho alto**.

12. El deporte es **importante**.
    STUDENT: Es **un deporte importante**.

17. La muchacha es **rica**.

18. La camisa es **bonita**. etc.

In Russian a similar drill is used:

1. Ребенок счастлив.
   STUDENT: Он счастливый ребенок.[4]

9. Кровать мала.
   STUDENT: Это маленькая кровать.[5]

19. Пирожное вкусно.
   STUDENT: Это вкусное пирожное.[6]

[4] The child is happy.
He's a happy child. (*masculine noun*)
[5] The bed is small.
It's a small bed. (*feminine noun*)
[6] The cake is tasty.
It's a tasty cake. (*neuter noun*)

In German and other highly inflected languages the oral drill is just as effective, although there must be many more pairs to cover all the possible agreements:

1. Dort steht ein Mann. Er ist **alt.**
   STUDENT: Dort steht **ein alter Mann.**

7. Dort steht ein Kind. Es ist **klein.**
   STUDENT: Dort steht **ein kleines Kind.**

70. Ich habe den Bleistift. Er ist **gut.**
    STUDENT: Ich habe den **guten** Bleistift.
    (For agreement in the accusative, weak endings)

78. Hans hat das Buch. Es ist **schwer.**
    STUDENT: Hans hat das **schwere** Buch.
    (For agreement in the accusative case, neuter nouns)

86. Wir sehen die Frau. Sie ist **schön.**
    STUDENT: Wir sehen die **schöne** Frau. u.s.w.
    (Accusative case, feminine noun, weak ending)

Adjectives may be compared by using the analogy system:

Compare the persons and things mentioned, using **plus . . . que:**

1. Georges est petit. Et Robert?
   STUDENT: Robert est **plus petit** que Georges.

2. Georges est intelligent. Et Robert?
   STUDENT: Robert est **plus intelligent** que Georges.

. . .

8. La cuisine est **grande.** Et le salon?
   STUDENT: Le salon est **plus grand** que la cuisine.

9. Le père est **âgé.** Et le grand-père?
   STUDENT: Le grand-père est **plus âgé** que le père.

This drill is modified to be used with **moins . . . que** (less . . . than) and **aussi . . . que** (just as . . . as), using the same general system.

2. Adverbs. Adverbs must be taught in conjunction with verbs, adjectives, other adverbs, and (as adverbs of quantity) with nouns. Some ways of presenting drills for these purposes are:

Restate, inserting the adverb in its proper place:

1. **toujours** / Robert travaille dans le jardin.
   STUDENT: Robert travaille **toujours** dans le jardin.

2. **souvent** / Mon frère va au cinéma.
   STUDENT: Mon frère va **souvent** au cinéma.

3. **déjà**/Georges étudie dans le salon.
   STUDENT: Georges étudie **déjà** dans le salon.

80. **gestern** / Ich habe ihn nicht gesehen.
   STUDENT: Ich habe ihn **gestern** nicht gesehen.

81. **am Montag** / Wir sind nach Hause gefahren.
   STUDENT: Wir sind **am Montag** nach Hause gefahren.

89. **vor zehn Minuten** / Er hat seinen Platz gefunden.
   STUDENT: Er hat seinen Platz **vor zehn Minuten** gefunden.

1. **Всегда** / Учитель работает.
   STUDENT: Учитель работает **всегда**.[7]

2. **Часто** / Я хожу в кино.
   STUDENT: Я хожу в кино **часто**.[8]

Word order in German may further be taught by use of this kind of drill:

Begin each sentence with the adverb:

1. Der Brunnen ist **tief**.
   STUDENT: **Tief** ist der Brunnen.

2. Wir wollen **jetzt** beginnen.
   STUDENT: **Jetzt** wollen wir beginnen.

8. Ein schönes Denkmal steht **vor dem Rathaus**.
   STUDENT: **Vor dem Rathaus** steht ein schönes Denkmal.

For showing use of adverbs with adjectives:

[7] Always / The teacher works.
   The teacher always works.
[8] Often / I go to the movies.
   I often go to the movies.

Restate, incorporating **très** (*and, in succeeding runs through the exercise,* **extrêmement, bien**) *in the statement:*

1. Jean est heureux.
   STUDENT: Jean est très heureux.

2. Marie est intelligente.

6. Nous sommes fatigués.

Such a drill is easily adapted to Spanish (**muy,** etc.), German (**sehr**), and other languages taught in the schools.

To show the use of adverbs of quantity, the student responds with a fixed increment—in this case a predetermined adverb:

Answer, using **beaucoup de** (*and in successive runs through the exercise,* **assez de, trop de, plusieurs**):

1. Avez-vous des livres?
   STUDENT: Oui, j'ai **beaucoup de** livres. (first drill)
   STUDENT: Oui, j'ai **assez de** livres. (second drill)
   STUDENT: Oui, j'ai **trop de** livres. (third drill)
   STUDENT: Oui, j'ai **plusieurs** livres. (fourth drill)

2. Avez-vous des chats?

3. Avez-vous des idées?

19. Jean a-t-il de l'argent?

3. Articles and Contractions. For the teaching of articles, contractions, and for incidental drilling on the gender of nouns, an open-end mutation drill is used:

TAPE: Repeat: à
STUDENT: **à**

TAPE: la maison
STUDENT: **à la** maison

TAPE: la gare
STUDENT: **à la** gare

TAPE: la bibliothèque
STUDENT: **à la** bibliothèque

TAPE: l'école
STUDENT: à l'école

TAPE: l'université
STUDENT: à l'université
(About 8 more with l'.)

TAPE: Repeat: au   [CONTRACTION INTRODUCED]
STUDENT: au

TAPE: le musée
STUDENT: au musée

TAPE: le jardin
STUDENT: au jardin

TAPE: les maisons   [PLURAL INTRODUCED]
STUDENT: aux maisons

TAPE: les gares
STUDENT: aux gares

TAPE: Repeat: de   [NEW PREPOSITION INTRODUCED]
STUDENT: de

TAPE: la maison
STUDENT: de la maison, etc.

TAPE: le musée
STUDENT: du musée

TAPE: le jardin
STUDENT: du jardin, etc.

Other prepositions are gradually introduced, but those having contractions must be stressed.

TAPE: Repeat: a
STUDENT: a

TAPE: la escuela
STUDENT: a la escuela

TAPE: la iglesia
STUDENT: a la iglesia

TAPE: el centro
STUDENT: **al** centro

TAPE: el cine
STUDENT: **al** cine

TAPE: el padre
STUDENT: **al** padre

TAPE: Repeat: de
STUDENT: **de**

TAPE: la niña
STUDENT: **de la** niña

TAPE: el padre
STUDENT: **del** padre, etc.

In such highly inflected languages as German and Russian, the drill on prepositions is even more important because of the use of cases:

TAPE: Repeat: mit
STUDENT: **mit**

TAPE: der Bleistift
STUDENT: **mit dem** Bleistift

TAPE: der Arm
STUDENT: **mit dem** Arm

TAPE: die Hand
STUDENT: **mit der** Hand

TAPE: das Mädchen
STUDENT: **mit dem** Mädchen

TAPE: bei   [NEW PREPOSITION, SAME CASE]
STUDENT: **bei dem** Mädchen

TAPE: für   [NEW PREPOSITION, ACCUSATIVE]
STUDENT: **für das** Mädchen

TAPE: die Mütter   [SAME PREPOSITION, PLURAL]
STUDENT: **für die** Mütter, u.s.w.

These examples are not full enough to show the complete patterning, but in general, at least eight pairs of the same type are retained before changing to a new noun gender, a new preposition, a new case. These are open-end substitutions, since a change may be made in the preposition *or* in the noun.

4. Comparisons. Both quantities and qualities may be compared. Some ways of comparing adjectives (qualities) have already appeared under the heading *Adjectives*. Model oral drills for comparisons are shown below:

> *Compare, using* **más:**
>
> 1. Este reloj es bonito.
>   STUDENT: Mi reloj es **más** bonito.
>
> 2. Esta camisa es fea.
>   STUDENT: Mi camisa es **más** fea.
>
> 80. Mein Bruder ist klein.
>   STUDENT: Mein Bruder ist **kleiner als ich.**
>
> 81. Renata ist schön.
>   STUDENT: Renata ist **schöner als ich.**
>
> 90. Eine Sekunde ist kurz.
>   STUDENT: Eine Sekunde ist **kürzer als** eine Minute.

For teaching the superlative form, the following fixed increment drill is suggested:

> 1. Alain a une maison intéressante.
>   STUDENT: Alain a la maison **la plus intéressante** *de la ville.*
>
> 22. Alain a une belle auto.
>   STUDENT: Alain a **la plus belle** auto *de la ville.*

For the comparison of quantities (nouns):

> 1. J'ai plusieurs livres.
>   STUDENT: J'ai **plus de** livres **que vous.**
>
> 2. J'ai beaucoup d'argent.
>   STUDENT: J'ai **plus** d'argent **que vous.** (first drill)
>   STUDENT: J'ai **moins** d'argent **que vous.** (second drill)
>   STUDENT: J'ai **autant** d'argent **que vous.** (third drill)

5. Negation of Verbs. Negation is easily drilled by providing a series of simple positive statements for the student to make negative:

> 1. Je travaille. (STUDENT: Je **ne** travaille **pas.**)
>
> 50. J'ai travaillé. (STUDENT: Je **n'ai pas** travaillé.)
>
> 80. Robert partira. (STUDENT: Robert **ne** partira **pas.**)

> 1. Я знаю. (STUDENT: Я не знаю.)
>
> 2. Я работаю. (STUDENT: Я не работаю.)

Using alternate negative terms such as **ne . . . jamais** (never), **ne . . . plus** (no longer):

> 1. Je travaille. (STUDENT: Je **ne** travaille **jamais.**)
>
> 50. J'ai travaillé. (STUDENT: Je **n'ai** jamais **travaillé.**)

Negation of infinitives:

> 26. Alain me demande de fermer la fenêtre.
> STUDENT: Alain me demande de **ne pas** fermer la fenêtre.
>
> 27. Je préfère étudier ce soir.
> STUDENT: Je préfère **ne pas** étudier ce soir.

Negation with object pronouns:

> 1. Alain me la donne.
> STUDENT: Alain **ne** me la donne **pas.**
>
> 50. Donnez-le-moi.
> STUDENT: **Ne** me le donnez **pas.**

For all negation drills, a simple positive statement can be presented for the student to change to the negative. In addition, he may be asked questions to be answered in the negative:

> 1. Avez-vous beaucoup d'argent?
> STUDENT: Non, je **n'ai pas** beaucoup d'argent.
>
> 8. Robert a-t-il des sœurs?
> STUDENT: Non, il **n'a pas** de sœurs.

Since the latter drill requires more changes than the simple mutation drills that preceded, it would be used only after the principle of negation and verb forms had been mastered.

6. Partitives. The partitive construction in the case of French (and other languages requiring the partitive) may be approached with an oral fixed increment drill such as the following:

Answer, using **il y a . . . sur la table:**   [PARTITIVE REQUIRED]

   1. J'aime les fleurs.
      STUDENT: Il y a **des fleurs** sur la table.

   2. J'aime les livres.
      STUDENT: Il y a **des livres** sur la table.

Answer, stating that the thing mentioned is **useful:**

  67. Voilà des livres.
      STUDENT: **Les livres** sont utiles.   [GENERAL ARTICLE]

  68. Voilà des crayons.
      STUDENT: **Les crayons** sont utiles.

Say that Marie has the things mentioned:

  80. Le talent est utile.
      STUDENT: Marie a **du talent.**   [PARTITIVE REQUIRED]

181. L'argent est utile.
      STUDENT: Marie a **de l'argent.**

Ask for the item mentioned:

100. J'aime la viande.
      STUDENT: Donnez-moi **de la viande.**

112. J'aime les fruits.
      STUDENT: Donnez-moi **des fruits.**

120. J'aime le vin.
      STUDENT: Donnez-moi **du vin.**

121. J'aime le café.
      STUDENT: Donnez-moi **du café.**

Notice that the student response is set up by establishing a consistent pattern. For example, stimulus number 112 above would be followed by several more plural nouns, all calling for the *des* response. Then (as shown by number 120) a new phase would be introduced, calling for a *du* response. Since the type of drill to be recorded will be the *anticipation drill* (described in full in the next chapter), the exercise will be self-correcting and the student will know when he has failed to recognize the transition point. The second time through the drill he will be alert to respond accurately to new stimulus patterns.

7. **Pronouns.** Subject and object pronouns are the most common things to be taught. Students have to learn to select the correct form, and to place that word in the correct position. Subject pronouns are easily elicited by substitution drills:

    1. **Jean** va au cinéma. (STUDENT: **Il** va au cinéma.)

    8. **Marie** va au cinéma. (STUDENT: **Elle** va au cinéma.)

   16. **Jean et Marie** arrivent. (STUDENT: **Ils** arrivent.)

   80. **Hans** geht ins Kino. (STUDENT: **Er** geht ins Kino.)

   85. **Das Kind** geht ins Kino. (STUDENT: **Es** geht ins Kino.)

   94. **Meine Eltern** sprechen Deutsch. (STUDENT: **Sie** sprechen Deutsch.)

    1. **Иван** идет в кино.
      STUDENT: **Он** идет в кино.

    9. **Мария** идет в кино.
      STUDENT: **Она** идет в кино.

To elicit direct object pronouns, a substitution drill can again be used:

    1. El profesor lee **la lección.**
      STUDENT: El profesor **la** lee.

    2. La madre cierra **la puerta.**
      STUDENT: La madre **la** cierra.

   56. Robert regarde **le dictionnaire.**
      STUDENT: Robert **le** regarde.

   57. Robert ferme **le livre.**
      STUDENT: Robert **le** ferme.

65. Albert quitte **la maison.**
STUDENT: Albert **la** quitte.

1. Ich sehe **den Hund.**
STUDENT: Ich sehe **ihn.**

4. Ich sehe **die Katze.**
STUDENT: Ich sehe **sie.**

8. Ich sehe **das Haus.**
STUDENT: Ich sehe **es.**

15. Ich sehe **meine Freunde.**
STUDENT: Ich sehe **sie.**

1. Я вижу стол.
STUDENT: Я его вижу.[9]

9. Я вижу книгу.
STUDENT: Я её вижу.[10]

To elicit indirect object pronouns, a substitution drill:

1. Robert parle **à la concierge.**
STUDENT: Robert **lui** parle.

2. Robert parle **à Georges.**
STUDENT: Robert **lui** parle.

9. Robert parle **à ses parents.**
STUDENT: Robert **leur** parle.

1. Roberto habla **a su padre.**
STUDENT: Roberto **le** habla.

9. Roberto habla **a su madre.**
STUDENT: Roberto **le** habla.

17. Roberto habla **a sus padres.**
STUDENT: Roberto **les** habla.

80. Ich zeige es **dem Vater.**
STUDENT: Ich zeige es **ihm.**

---

[9] I see the table. I see it. (*m.*)
[10] I see the book. I see it. (*f.*)

88. Ich zeige es **der Mutter.**
    STUDENT: Ich zeige es **ihr.**

98. Ich zeige es **dem Kind.**
    STUDENT: Ich zeige es **ihm.**

1. Игорь разговаривает с полицейским.
   STUDENT: Игорь разговаривает с ним.[11]

7. Игорь разговаривает со старой женщиной.
   STUDENT: Игорь разговаривает с ней.[12]

To elicit substitution and correct placement of two pronouns in a single sentence, a double substitution drill:

1. Robert donne le *livre à sa sœur.*
   STUDENT: Robert le *lui* donne.

7. Robert donne les *livres à ses amis.*
   STUDENT: Robert les *leur* donne.

17. Nous rendons les **cahiers** *au professeur.*
    STUDENT: Nous les *lui* rendons.

80. Er gibt **seiner Schwester** *das Buch.*
    STUDENT: Er gibt *es* ihr.

85. Er gibt **seinem Bruder** *das Buch.*
    STUDENT: Er gibt *es* ihm.

89. Er gibt **seinen Eltern** *das Buch.*
    STUDENT: Er gibt *es* ihnen.

93. Er gibt **seiner Schwester** *den Bleistift.*
    STUDENT: Er gibt *ihn* ihr.

97. Er gibt **seinem Bruder** *den Bleistift.*
    STUDENT: Er gibt *ihn* ihm.

To elicit disjunctive pronouns in French, a substitution drill:

1. Jean est allé au cinéma **avec Marie.**
   STUDENT: Jean est allé au cinéma **avec elle.**

[11] Igor is talking to the policeman.
   Igor is talking to him.
[12] Igor is talking to the old woman.
   Igor is talking to her.

8. Jean est allé à la plage **avec Henri.**
   STUDENT: Jean est allé à la plage **avec lui.**

12. Robert est allé à Paris **avec ses parents.**
    STUDENT: Robert est allé à Paris **avec eux.**

1. Êtes-vous allé au cinéma **avec Alain?**
   STUDENT: Oui, Alain et **moi,** nous sommes allés au cinéma.

20. Qui est allé au cinéma **avec Robert?**
    STUDENT: **C'est moi** qui suis allé au cinéma **avec lui.**

21. Qui a parlé français **avec mes sœurs?**
    STUDENT: **C'est moi** qui ai parlé français **avec elles.**

Relative pronouns can be elicited by use of a *paired sentence* drill. Two short sentences are given orally; the student combines them into a single sentence containing a relative pronoun.

1. Mi padre es profesor. Enseña la historia.
   STUDENT: Mi padre, **quien** es profesor, enseña la historia.

10. Alain aime les fleurs. Alain a un jardin.
    STUDENT: Alain, **qui** aime les fleurs, a un jardin.
    (*subject pronoun used*)

30. Voilà le café. Nous fréquentons le café.
    STUDENT: Voilà le café **que** nous frequentons.
    (*direct object pronoun used*)

40. Voilà le stylo. Nous écrivons avec le stylo.
    STUDENT: Voilà le stylo **avec lequel** nous écrivons.
    (*object of preposition*)

1. Der Mann ist alt. Der Mann wohnt hier.
   STUDENT: Der Mann, **der** hier wohnt, ist alt.

11. Ich sehe eine Uhr. Die Uhr ist alt.
    STUDENT: Ich sehe eine Uhr, **die** alt ist.

24. Der Wagen ist neu. Er kauft den Wagen.
    STUDENT: Der Wagen, **den** er kauft, ist neu.

The German drill can be continued to cover genitive and dative, singular and plural, as well as various forms of *welcher* instead of *der*. Afterwards, a similar drill can bring in relative pronouns following prepositions, including the *wo-* forms.

The pronoun **celui** (the one) can be elicited in French as follows:

Substitute the appropriate form of **celui** *for the repeated noun:*

57. Voilà mon livre et **le livre** d'Albert.
    STUDENT: Voilà mon livre et **celui** d'Albert.

65. Mon école est près de **l'école** de Georges.
    STUDENT: Mon école est près de **celle** de Georges.

Other pronouns, such as **y** and **en,** can be elicited by a simple substitution drill:

1. Alain va **à Paris.**
   STUDENT: Alain **y** va.

12. Robert pense **à ce problème.**
    STUDENT: Robert **y** pense.

20. Pierre a **de l'argent.**
    STUDENT: Pierre **en** a.

8. Government of Prepositions (Régimes). In languages whose grammar requires certain prepositions before infinitives, the pattern can be established as follows:

Complete the fragment with **hablar español:**

1. Yo quiero . . .
   STUDENT: Yo **quiero** hablar español.

2. Nos gusta . . .
   STUDENT: Nos **gusta** hablar español.
   (*several more examples requiring* **no** *preposition*)

9. Enrique empieza . . .
   STUDENT: Enrique **empieza a** hablar español.

10. Ana aprende . . .
    STUDENT: Ana **aprende a** hablar español.
    (*several more completions requiring* **a**)

18. Juan trata . . .
    STUDENT: Juan **trata de** hablar español.
    (*several more requiring* **de**)

Complete the fragment with **étudier le français:**

1. J'aime . . .
   STUDENT: **J'aime** étudier le français.   [FIXED INCREMENT]

2. Nous voulons . . .
   STUDENT: Nous **voulons** étudier le français.

12. Georges commence . . .
    STUDENT: Georges **commence** à étudier le français.

13. Georges continue . . .
    STUDENT: Georges **continue** à étudier le français.

20. Alain cesse . . .
    STUDENT: Alain **cesse** d'étudier le français.

25. Essayez . . .
    STUDENT: **Essayez** d'étudier le français.

9. Verbs. Verb forms may be elicited (without recourse to simple repetition) through analogy drills. Questions are framed so as to force a particular answer containing the desired verb form. This technique has the advantage of having a conversational question-answer form such as might take place in real life:

1. Je change de train. Et vous?
   STUDENT: Je change aussi de train.

8. Je change de train. Et Robert?
   STUDENT: Robert change aussi de train.

11. Robert change de train. Et vos frères?
    STUDENT: Ils changent aussi de train.
    (*The sequence of No. 11, and the six following in its pattern, teaches the student that there is no difference in pronunciation between the third-person singular and third-person plural verb forms for this type of verb.*)

32. Robert arrive demain. Et nous?
    STUDENT: Nous arrivons demain.

40. Marie a l'air fatigué. Et moi?
    STUDENT: Vous avez l'air fatigué.

1. María entiende el español. ¿Y Vds.?
   STUDENT: Nosotros entendemos el español.

8. Pablo va a la iglesia. ¿Y sus amigos?
STUDENT: Sus amigos van a la iglesia.

1. Олег поднимает книгу. А ты?
STUDENT: Я поднимаю книгу.[13]

9. Олег смотрит на дом. А мы?
STUDENT: Мы смотрим на дом.[14]

12. Олег думает о девушке. А мы?
STUDENT: Мы думаем о девушке.[15]

Paired sentences are often useful. In the following drill on the use of the present participle, the student joins both sentences into a single one:

1. Renée **préparait** le déjeuner. Elle s'est coupé le doigt.
STUDENT: **En préparant** le déjeuner, Renée s'est coupé le doigt.

2. Le professeur **regardait** l'élève. Il lui a posé une question.
STUDENT: **En regardant** l'élève, le professeur lui a posé une question.

Paired sentences can be used to show tense couplings, as in the French interplay of the imperfect and passé composé in narration in the past, in conditional sentences, in the use of the subjunctive, and the like.

The following pairs are in the present tense. The second action is dependent upon the circumstance described in the first sentence. Join these pairs into conditional sentences beginning with **si:**

46. (a) Il fait beau. (b) Je **vais** en ville.
STUDENT: **S'il** fait beau, j'**irai** en ville.
(*also usable for conditional tense*)
STUDENT: **S'il faisait** beau, j'**irais** en ville.

47. (a) Il fait mauvais. (b) Je reste chez moi.
STUDENT: **S'il** fait mauvais, je **resterai** chez moi.
STUDENT: **S'il faisait** mauvais, je **resterais** chez moi.

[13] Oleg is picking up the book. And you?
I am picking up the book.
[14] Oleg is looking at the house. How about us?
We are looking at the house.
[15] Oleg is thinking about the girl. How about us?
We are thinking about the girl.

53. (a) Nous avons le temps. (b) Nous allons au ballet.

To teach the use of the imperfect and passé composé in narration in the past, paired sentences might be arranged as follows:

1. (a) Alain étudie. (b) Je rentre.
   STUDENT: Alain **étudiait** quand je **suis rentré.**

2. (a) Robert travaille. (b) Henri arrive.
   STUDENT: Robert **travaillait** quand Henri **est arrivé.**

To teach the subjunctive, fixed increment drills are useful. The student is asked to prefix a fixed expression calling for the subjunctive:

Prefix each fragment with **Il faut que:**

1. . . . j'arrive à l'heure.
   STUDENT: Il faut que **j'arrive** à l'heure.

12. . . . je **finis** la leçon.
    STUDENT: Il faut que **je finisse** la leçon.

30. . . . Robert **va** en ville.
    STUDENT: Il faut que **Robert aille** en ville.

Prefix each fragment with **Es necesario que:**

1. . . . Elena **estudia** el francés.
   STUDENT: Es necesario que Elena **estudie** el francés.

8. . . . Juan **va** al centro.
   STUDENT: Es necesario que Juan **vaya** al centro.

9. . . . María **termina** la lección.
   STUDENT: Es necesario que María **termine** la lección.

After the present tense of verbs has been taught, a drill consisting of present tense statements can be used for a mutation drill. The student merely changes the present tense to another tense being learned, adding an adverb (like *yesterday, tomorrow*) to justify the new tense:

Change to the passé composé:

1. Alain **commande** un bon dîner.
   STUDENT: Alain **a commandé** un bon dîner hier.

9. Nous **finissons** la leçon.
   STUDENT: Nous **avons fini** la leçon hier.

12. Mes amis **sortent** de la maison.
    STUDENT: Mes amis **sont sortis** de la maison hier.

Change to the future tense:

1. Alain **commande** un bon dîner.
   STUDENT: Alain **commandera** un bon dîner. etc.

Change to the preterite: (or *to the future*)

1. Pablo **llega** a las siete.
   STUDENT: Pablo **llegó** a las siete ayer.

7. Juan **parte** para Madrid.
   STUDENT: Juan **partió** para Madrid ayer.

9. Yo **salgo** de la casa a las cinco.
   STUDENT: Yo **salí** de la casa a las cinco ayer.

Change to the past:

1. Я иду в школу.
   STUDENT: Я ходил в школу вчера.[16]

12. Я говорю с учителем.
    STUDENT: Я говорил с учителем вчера.[17]

18. Борис открывает окно.
    STUDENT: Борис открывал окно вчера.[18]

Students should be prepared in class for new laboratory drills. The teacher can present some examples from the drill, give instructions concerning correct position of the vocal organs to produce new sounds, and be certain that all members of the class understand the system being used in the drill. The class can simulate laboratory performance for a few minutes with the teacher playing the part of the master tape. Only a few minutes of this are needed, and the routine of learning can take place in the laboratory.

[16] I go to school.
I went to school yesterday.
[17] I speak to the teacher.
I spoke to the teacher yesterday.
[18] Boris opens the window.
Boris opened the window yesterday.

17. I see the nurse. (STUDENT: I see **her**.)

Again there are eight pairs (numbers 9 through 16) eliciting the direct object pronoun *him,* and eight pairs (numbers 17 through 24) eliciting the direct object pronoun *her.* This would conclude the teaching phase of the drill, because we stated that the purpose of the drill was to teach just these three important direct object pronouns. The term *pattern* should now become apparent in its use with regard to oral drills: it means that sufficient examples (here, eight) of a consistent nature are given as a solid block of work. After this segment is completed, the next variation is introduced.

The **testing phase** follows the teaching phase immediately and without announcement that it is a special part of the drill. In our example, the last pair in the teaching phase was 24, and therefore starting with number 25 the testing portion is presented. The testing phase is simply a sampling in random order of the patterned **segments** of the teaching phase. Pairs are now given calling for *it, him, her* in the response in mixed order. Some of the pairs are directly drawn from the teaching phase, and some new ones, capable of being correctly solved on the basis of the teaching phase, are also introduced. The length of the testing phase is open to the discretion of the instructor, but it is recommended that it be from one-third to one-fourth the length of the teaching phase. Our full drill for the example we have been using would be composed of the following:

PATTERN DRILL: English 1

Anticipation Mode (4-phase), Substitution Type

PURPOSE: Teaching use of direct object pronouns **it, him, her.**

	ITEM	SEGMENT (PAIRS)	TOTALS
TEACHING PHASE	**it**	8	
	him	8	
	her	8	
			24
TESTING PHASE	**it, him, her,** *mixed*	10	
TOTAL NUMBER OF PAIRS			34

Using the rule-of-thumb that pattern drills can be recorded (including pauses required by the anticipation mode described later on) at the rate of about five pairs per minute, this tape would last about seven minutes ($34 \div 5$). Such a drill is short enough to allow a student to go through the drill at least twice during a laboratory period. It is assumed that the student will miss many of the responses on the first hearing, and that he will improve greatly on the second. A third hearing should bring perfect results, but if not, further hearings should be required. Frequent reviews are advisable even after the student is able to make perfect responses to the drill.

How long should a drill be? This depends upon the length of a laboratory period, and upon how complicated the problem presented is. If the student is in the laboratory for about 40 minutes, and we desire that he hear and respond to the drill at least twice during the period, the tape should be kept to a maximum of 15 minutes. Time must be allowed for arrival and departure, adjustment of equipment, and other similar activities. If the tape is only seven minutes in length, as is our English 1 drill above, and the period is 40 minutes, a second pattern drill could be introduced to teach the use of the direct objects *us, you, them,* to make the total material about 15 minutes in length.

Since the length of the laboratory period is usually fixed by the school schedule, the factors that are variable for the teacher are (1) the length of the drill and (2) the number of times the drill is to be repeated during the period. The teacher must often subdivide the instructional material to make a drill of correct length, just as the direct objects in English were not *all* presented in our sample drill. In German, for example, the definite article has six different forms (*der, des, dem, den, die, das*), but these are used sixteen different ways because of the genders and cases involved. An analysis of the number of pairs needed to teach the definite article in German would give us this:

PATTERN DRILL: German 1

Anticipation Mode (4-phase), Open-end Mutation

PURPOSE: Teaching **der, die, das, die,** all cases.

		SEGMENT	
	ITEM	(PAIRS)	TOTALS
TEACHING PHASE *m.*	**der** (*nom.*)	8	
	den (*acc.*)	8	
	dem (*dat.*)	8	
	des (*gen.*)	8	

	ITEM	SEGMENT (PAIRS)	TOTALS
TEACHING PHASE *n.*	das (*nom.*)	8	
	das (*acc.*)	8	
	dem (*dat.*)	8	
	des (*gen.*)	8	
			32
f.	die (*nom.*)	8	
	die (*acc.*)	8	
	der (*dat.*)	8	
	der (*gen.*)	8	
			32
pl.	die (*nom.*)	8	
	die (*acc.*)	8	
	den (*dat.*)	8	
	der (*gen.*)	8	
			32
Total Pairs, Teaching Phase			128
TESTING PHASE (⅓ of 128)			42
TOTAL NUMBER OF PAIRS FOR DRILL			170

This drill would last about 34 minutes, and would allow no repetition. In such a case it would be best to subdivide the work into separate drills— one on the nominative and accusative of (say) masculine and neuter nouns, one on use of the dative after certain prepositions, etc.—making *several* drills to cover the material. With really complicated material involving many forms, such subdividing is essential.

Sometimes the suggested sequence of eight examples in a given segment is insufficient. For instance, there are 15 prepositions in German requiring the accusative case of nouns under certain circumstances. Since the student must be familiar with all of these, eight examples of accusative case responses would not be enough. The number of examples must be increased to accommodate such a circumstance—ohne (*without*) should be used about eight times with a masculine singular noun in the accusative, then eight with a feminine singular noun in the accusative, and so on. This can lead to long laboratory work, but the complication of German justifies it, and the results will be most gratifying.

In summary, pattern drills consist of a **teaching phase** and a **testing phase**. The teaching phase is divided into consistent **segments** of about eight pairs each to establish a pattern. The number of segments depends upon the objective of the drill. The objective should include a small enough number of points to allow the drill to last from two or three minutes for a simple objective to 15 minutes. The maximum time is determined by the length of the laboratory period. A drill should be heard twice at least, and time must be allowed for adjustment of equipment. If the laboratory period is 30 minutes, allow five to seven minutes for getting settled and for closing station. The remaining time (23-25 minutes) is divided by two (for two hearings) to determine the available listening time (about 12 minutes of drills in this case).

To keep the laboratory interesting and challenging, two or more drills of different natures might be combined to use up the available time. The seven-minute drill on the English direct objects *it, him, her,* might be followed by a five-minute drill on an entirely different problem, like the verb *to have,* to make up the laboratory program for that particular period. The seven-minute drill would be heard twice, then the five-minute drill twice. The following laboratory period would review—perhaps by playing only the testing portions of each of these two tapes—before presenting a new drill.

11. Anticipation Mode. Oral drills are recorded (or used "live" in class) in the anticipation mode. This name is applied to the mechanical arrangement of pauses and stimuli. It is a four-phase arrangement *for each pair:*

1. The **stimulus** is spoken by the teacher.
2. PAUSE. The student responds, anticipating the correct answer about to be given.
3. The **correct response** is given by the teacher.
4. PAUSE. The student repeats the correct response.

Phases 2 and 4 are simply pauses of a length appropriate for the student response. Phases 1 and 3 are the *pairs* spoken by the teacher or native speaker employed. Obviously the script used for recording need contain 1 and 3 only—the stimulus and the correct response. The anticipation mode may be represented graphically by showing a piece of dual-channel tape thus:

MASTER	STIMULUS		CORRECT RESPONSE	
STUDENT		ATTEMPTED RESPONSE		REPETITION
Phase 1	2		3	

Fig. 1: Anticipation Drill

Phases 3 and 4 compose a simple repetition drill of the old and well-known sort. The anticipation drill has many advantages. It requires active thinking on the part of the student rather than ordinary mimicry, since the stimulus (phase 1) and response (phase 2) are not the same. This puts the language exchange on the basis of context and conversational style. The drill is a self-correcting one; that is, it is not necessary for the teacher to monitor the drill to point out errors. This is because the student's response (phase 2) is compared immediately with the correct response (phase 3), and if there is a difference, the contrast is striking; the student knows he has erred and immediately repeats the correct response in phase 4. The repetition is done even though the student may have given the correct reply in phase 2, because further practice drives the point home and gives additional practice in correct structure and pronunciation.

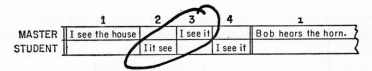

Fig. 2: Self-Correcting Feature: Contrast

The anticipation mode is used for all drills suggested in this book. There are various kinds of patterns that can be fitted into this mode, and the discussion of them will follow shortly.

12. Tapescripts. The script for an oral drill should be written so as to facilitate the recording (or class use) of the drill. A particular format should be standardized for the laboratory so that, regardless of the identity of the person making the tape, certain information always appears in the same order on the tape. The students will then fall quickly into the routine of the laboratory and will not have to figure out each new tape as it is heard. If the student has learned how to use an anticipation drill during the first week, no explanations other than "Anticipation Drill, Substitution," need be given on the tape itself, and much time can be saved for actual speaking of the foreign language.

The script consists of pairs, phases 1 and 3 of the anticipation drill:

      1. Je vois la maison. #
         Je la vois. #

1. La pluma es negra. ¿Y el lápiz? #
   El lápiz es negro. #

The sign # indicates to the speaker that a pause sufficiently long for the student's response must be allowed before reading the next line of the script. The technique is to speak at normal native speed. To be sure that sufficient time is allowed for student responses, say the response silently *twice* before reading the next line.

It is essential that normal native speed and pronunciation be used as soon as possible. Artificial slowing on the part of the instructor is permissible during the earliest phases of presentation of individual sounds of the language, but this procedure should be abandoned as soon as practicable. Gradual and early transition to native speed, both in understanding and in speaking, will enable students to understand and communicate with native speakers. Failure to recognize this fact will handicap students.

A standard format for recorded drills is given in § 14 (at the end of this chapter) after various kinds of drills have been defined. Teachers should be supplied with a standard first page for the tapescripts to be used in their laboratory. These standard pages could be similar to that shown in Fig. 11.

13. Types of Drills. Drills may be classified as analogy drills, mutation drills, fixed increment drills, paired sentence drills, narration drills, and exploded drills. Most of these drills were demonstrated in Chapter II under grammatical categories. In this section each kind of drill will be defined, and its general area of usefulness indicated. Models for the patterns will be shown.

A. Analogy Drill. An analogy drill elicits the use of words in a new way, but this new way is controlled by a fragmentary question attached to the stimulus. It is useful for teaching adjective agreement, verb forms, and other inflections. Models are given below:

(ADJECTIVES) 1. This house is **big**. How about the garage?
   The garage is **big** (too).

2. Cette dame est **charmante**. Et ce monsieur?
   Ce monsieur est **charmant**.

3. La señora es **alta**. ¿Y el señor?
   El señor es **alto**.

(VERBS)   1. **I'm going** to the movies. How about John?
             John's going to the movies (too).

             2. **Robert finit** la leçon. Et vous?
             Je finis la leçon.

             3. **María entiende** el español. ¿Y Vds.?
             Nosotros entendemos el español.

Various forms of verbs can be elicited by use of the correct question fragment. This drill has the advantage of a conversation-like context.

B. Mutation Drill. A mutation drill calls for a change or substitution in the stimulus, leaving some of the stimulus as it was. This is, therefore, a repetition with a slight change. Mutation drills can be used for negation, word-order, pronouns, adverbs, contractions, numbers, and vocabulary drills. Models:

(NEGATION)   1. Bill **speaks** Russian.
             Bill **doesn't speak** Russian.

             2. Je **travaille.**
             Je **ne** travaille **pas.**

             3. Él canta.
             Él **no** canta.

(PRONOUNS,   1. We like **books.**
WORD-ORDER: We like **them.**
Substitution)

             2. Je cherche **mon dictionnaire.**
             Je **le** cherche.

             3. Ich sehe **den Hund.**
             Ich sehe **ihn.**

(ADVERBS)   1. **already.** He's gone home.
             He's gone home **already.**

             2. **déjà.** Elle est partie.
             Elle est **déjà** partie.

             3. **schon.** Er ist hier.
             Er ist **schon** hier.

(NUMBERS: 1. Does your car have **three** wheels?
Substitution No, it has **four** wheels.
of Next Higher
Number) 2. Avez-vous **huit** dollars?
Non, j'ai **neuf** dollars.

Open-end mutation drills are those in which a substitution or change may be made in one of two places, and the student must be alert to make the correct change.

1. Repeat: I see a cat.
   I see **a cat.**

2. a dog
   I see **a dog.**

3. a professor
   I see **a professor.**

4. We   [NEW SUBJECT]
   We see a professor.

5. a friend
   We see **a friend.**

6. have   [NEW VERB]
   We **have** a friend.

7. a book
   We have **a book.**

8. Robert   [NEW SUBJECT]
   Robert has a book. etc.

A sample open-end mutation may be found for foreign languages in the preceding chapter, under the treatment of articles and contractions, pages 16-18. Not only structure, verbs, and vocabulary, but also mental alertness and awareness of meaning are taught in this way.

If a mutation drill is of the substitution type, it is advisable to use the term *Substitution Drill* in presenting the drill to the students. If it is for negation, call it a *Negation Drill,* and so on. The number drill is difficult as it stands, for it requires a change in subject and verb as well as a number change and a possessive change. It could be simplified for early presentation to the mutation drill as follows:

1. Robert has **three** books. #
   Robert has **four** books. #

2. Robert has **four** pencils. #
   Robert has **five** pencils. # etc.

Mutation drills are very useful for teaching contractions (and incidentally genders of nouns and basic pronunciation) in the early stages of instruction.

The teaching of new verb tenses is accomplished by mutation drills. A patterned list of simple statements in the present tense is given as a stimulus, and the student makes a single change. He is instructed to change the verb to the new tense, often adding an adverb for justification of the tense:

1. John **arrives.** #   [TO PAST]
   John **arrived yesterday.** #

2. Alain **part** pour Paris. #   [TO PAST]
   Alain **est parti** pour Paris **hier.** #

3. Pablo **llega** a las siete. #   [TO FUTURE]
   Pablo **llegará** a las siete **mañana.** #

The same sentences in the present can be used, as the models indicate, to teach all newly introduced tenses.

C. Fixed Increment Drill. A fixed increment drill consists of a fragmentary stimulus and a standard phrase (the fixed increment) that the student combines with it. This drill is useful in teaching the subjunctive, and the use of prepositions before infinitives. Models:

(SUBJUNCTIVE) *Prefix each fragment with* **It's preferable that:**

1. . . . Robert **goes** to town.
   It's preferable that Robert **go** to town.

Prefix each fragment with **Il faut que:**

2. . . . **je vais** en ville.
   Il faut que j'aille en ville.

Prefix each fragment with **Es necesario que:**

3. . . . Elena **estudia** el francés.
   Es necesario que Elena **estudie** el francés.

(RÉGIMES)   *Complete each fragment with* **study French:**

1. We like . . .
   We like **to study French.**

Complete each fragment with **étudier le français:**

2. Je commence . . .
   Je commence **à étudier le français.**

Other examples of fixed increment drills can be found on pages 29 (subjunctive) and 26 (régimes). Other increments can be used for variety without affecting the point being taught.

D. Paired Sentence Drill. A stimulus for a paired sentence drill consists of two short, easily remembered statements. The student responds by combining the two statements into a single statement in a predetermined way. This type of drill is best used for teaching relative pronouns, conditional sentences, tense linkages in narration, and present participles. Models:

(RELATIVE PRONOUNS)   1. The man is arriving. The man speaks French.
   The man **who is arriving** speaks French.

2. Alain a un jardin. Alain aime les fleurs.
   Alain, **qui a un jardin,** aime les fleurs.

(CONDITIONAL SENTENCE TENSE LINKAGES)   1. The weather is nice. I am going to town.
   If the weather is nice **I will go to** town.

or

If the weather **were** nice I **would go to town.**

(PRESENT PARTICIPLES)   1. Renée was cooking. She cut her finger.
   While cooking, Renée cut her finger.

(TENSE LINKAGES) 1. John is reading. Henry enters.
John was reading *when* Henry entered.

For further examples of paired sentence drill, see pages 14 (German adjectives), 25 (relative pronouns), and 28 (conditional sentences).

Because of the longer memory needed, paired sentences are among the more difficult drills. Students should be trained early in the course to retain full sentences and ideas in the foreign language; dictation is a good device for requiring this.

55. (a) Monsieur Corbeau est un oiseau noir.
    (b) Il est malhonnête.
    (c) Il vole un fromage.
    (d) Il perche sur un arbre.
    (e) Monsieur Renard est un animal sournois.
    (f) Il flatte le corbeau.
    (g) Le corbeau écoute ce que le renard lui dit.
    (h) Il ouvre un large bec pour chanter.
    (i) En ouvrant son bec il laisse tomber sa proie.
    (j) Le renard prend le fromage.
    (k) Maître Corbeau apprend sa leçon— mais trop tard.

Fig. 3: Visual Stimulus for Narration Drill *

E. Narration Drill. A narration drill is a story told in short, simple statements in the present tense. These statements are the stimuli, and the student responds by changing each statement for *past* narrative, selecting the appropriate tense. Sometimes the statement will simply be repeated, using the same tense as the stimulus; the student must know what tense to use, and how to form the tenses.

This is a more advanced elementary drill used for teaching the inter-

* Reproduced by permission of the publisher. Edward M. Stack, *Elementary Oral and Written French*, Oxford University Press, 1959.

play of tenses in past narration, as, for example, the use of the imperfect and passé composé in French. Visual aids can be synchronized with the stimuli by filmstrip or duplicated individual picture sheets. The drill gains by having an obvious plot and good continuity, and students may be required to tell the story, using the picture alone after they have used the drill sufficiently for good pronunciation, intonation, and speed.

Retell in the past, using the appropriate tense:

1. Monsieur Corbeau **est** un oiseau noir. #
   Monsieur Corbeau **était** un oiseau noir. #

2. Il **est** malhonnête. #
   Il **était** malhonnête. #

3. Il **vole** un fromage. #
   Il **a volé** un fromage. #

4. Il **perche** sur un arbre. #
   Il **a perché** sur un arbre. # etc.

F. Questions. Questions may be framed and put into the anticipation mode so that the answer is clear. Such drills may be used for verb forms, which can be patterned, and for isolated but useful phrases difficult to pattern, such as idioms and greetings. The latter are learned more by rote than by patterning. Models:

(VERB FORMS) 1. **Does John like books?** #
Yes, John likes books. #

2. **Allez-vous** au cinéma ce soir? #
Oui, **je vais** au cinéma ce soir. #

(IDIOMS) 1. Pourquoi voulez-vous dîner? #
J'ai faim. #

2. Pourquoi fermez-vous la fenêtre? #
J'ai froid. #

3. Pourquoi Jean va-t-il à la bibliothèque? #
Il a besoin d'un livre. #

(GREETINGS, COMMON EXPRESSIONS) 1. Comment allez-vous? #
Je vais bien, merci. #

2. Quel jour sommes-nous? #
Nous sommes lundi. #

As there are several possible answers to the idiom stimuli, some class preparation is needed. In any case the anticipation mode of presentation will give the expected answer, and the second hearing by the student will eliminate divergent answers.

G. Exploded Drill. More advanced students will benefit from the use of exploded drills. An exploded drill is derived from an integral unit of the foreign language—a newscast, a poem, a political address, an interview, a conversation, a play, a song—as recorded without· pauses for repetition. It is converted into an exploded drill by *inserting pauses* for student repetition, and this is done mechanically in the laboratory. The original recording is copied on tape (if it is originally on a disk or other form of record). This tape is called the master tape. The teacher listens to the recording and selects places suitable for a break, or pause. These breaks must be after a rather *short, sense-making group* of words that the student can remember easily.

The exploded drill can be made by using two tape recorders, one of which must have an instantaneous-stop lever. This machine will be called M (master), and the other machine, which will be making the new exploded tape, will be C. The **output** of M is connected to the **input** of C. A blank tape is loaded on C, and C is set to record.

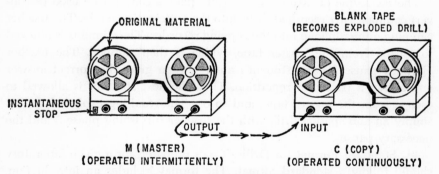

Fig. 4: Recorders Set for Making Exploded Drill

Now the master tape is loaded on M, and is made ready to play. We can stop the tape at any moment with the instant-stop lever. Set the blank tape in motion on C—it is now recording. Start M, letting out the first phrase and then stopping the tape movement. C continues to record silence while you repeat the phrase twice silently to allow the proper pause. Then release the stop lever, and let out another phrase. Stop again, repeat the phrase twice to time the pause, and then allow another phrase to escape from M. This process continues to the end of the selection. We then have a new exploded master on C, and the result is a drill usable in laboratory for teaching exact pronunciation, intonation, and speed.

Of course it would be possible to *read* a poem or speech phrase by phrase, leaving pauses, but the reader who does this anticipates the halting places, and the integrity of the total intonation pattern is lost. The exploded drill overcomes this difficulty.

Use the exploded drill for having students memorize things like the *Fables* of La Fontaine, for dictation, for preparing oral or written summaries of the contents of newscasts or stories. The first and best use is that of teaching excellent pronunciation and intonation through imitation.

Advanced students benefit from doing work ordinarily belonging to the teacher. A good student may be asked to listen to a newscast, poem, story, or speech in an integral recording. He will have to transcribe the material, decide where to place the pauses, and then actually make the exploded drill. This not only gives the student excellent practical experience, but relieves the teacher of some work. If there are several students who are good, let them work together as a committee on the transcript and division work.

The technique of artificially inserting pauses can also be used to convert commercially recorded drills into the anticipation mode. The teacher can plug a microphone into the copying recorder. The stimulus is allowed to escape from the master tape, which is then stopped. The teacher allows a pause for the student's answer, then gives the correct answer and allows a pause for repetition. Then the next stimulus is allowed to escape from the master tape, and so on. The resulting exploded drill is simply an anticipation drill, with the teacher furnishing phase 3 and the necessary pauses.

14. Standard Format for Drills. Tapes prepared for a given laboratory should follow a standard format. The format includes an introduction, presentation, and conclusion. Here is a sample format:

SPOKEN ON THE TAPE	REMARKS
Start.	This word is the first on the tape to make it easy to cue in. In use, the tape is threaded on a broadcasting tape deck, and when the word *start* is heard the move-

SPOKEN ON THE TAPE	REMARKS

[3-second silence]
Tape F2-07

ment of tape is halted. This assures the technician that the next sound to be heard is the beginning of the drill itself.

Pronounced: *Tape F two dash oh-seven.* Each tape bears an identifying number. The letter indicates the language, the next number is the course. After the dash is the serial number of the tape. (This system is explained in full in Section 20.)

Substitution Drill, Direct Object Pronouns.

Type of drill and general subject matter are announced.

Replace the direct object noun by the appropriate pronoun.

Instructions are kept *very* brief.

Join in as soon as you understand.

Standard challenge to the student to see and conform to the pattern set up in the drill.

Je vois la maison.
   [Pause]
Je la vois. [etc.]

Drill begins at once.

At the conclusion of the drill, the speaker announces, "End of tape F2-07" (using the actual number). This assures the user of the tape that there is no more, and that he need not continue to allow the tape to run. Spoken identification of the tape at beginning and end, in addition to markings on the reel and box, assures positive identification of tapes that have strayed from their proper boxes and reels.

The Language Laboratory

THE LANGUAGE laboratory is a special classroom for teaching foreign languages. It is equipped with individual private or semi-private stalls, or booths. The booths are connected into a network of audio wiring, the nerve center of which is the monitoring console. The monitoring console has a switchboard and tape decks, making it possible to play tapes and send the program to all or any combination of booths. The teacher at the console can listen in, or can have a two-way conversation with any student. The result is that recorded pattern drills may be broadcast to the students, and each student works in private as though he had a patient, unerring, unhesitating private tutor that never tired of repeating.

The language laboratory keeps a full class of students working and learning for the entire period. The teacher can monitor, correct, and grade twice as many students in the laboratory as was possible in a classroom recitation of the same duration. Classroom work complements laboratory work by preparing the student for the drills; classroom work becomes more flexible as students who have prepared in the laboratory come to class with good pronunciation, free of apprehension and with confidence in their handling of the language. The classroom is relieved of routine repetition drills and freed for flexible applications of the language.

This chapter and the two following it deal with the physical arrangement, routine, and administration of the language laboratory. Purposely omitted from the discussion are the mechanics of operating tape recorders and associated laboratory equipment. All the major brands differ from one another, and the operation of any particular brand of recorder or monitoring console is best learned in person, using the actual equipment. The most versatile type of laboratory now available is the dual-channel tape equipment, of which there are several brands. Less versatile laboratory equipment will often serve, and price is often the overriding factor in selection.

15. Equipment. In establishing a laboratory the first consideration is the equipment to be used. The main choice involves a decision as to mode of operation. There are two main modes of laboratory operation: the *broadcast* type and the *library* type. The first is most suitable for elementary and high school installations, where it is necessary to have an entire class working together. It is usually less expensive, too. The library mode is better suited to situations where students are more mature, or where students will work individually and at their own speed. Such is the case in most universities and colleges.

A. Broadcast Mode. The laboratory established on the broadcast mode has individual booths equipped with earphones, a microphone, and switches for program selection. There is usually not a tape-recording instrument at the booth. However, provision is made by most manufacturers for recording the student's performance remotely. If the student wants a criticism, or if the teacher wishes to use the recording for grading or helping the individual student, a recorder is simply switched into the circuit to a given booth.

The master tape containing the drill is placed on a central unit (the *console*), proper switches set, and when the tape is started, the drill is broadcast to all booths in the circuit. Students all work at the same speed, give the responses, and hear both themselves and the master in their earphones. Selected students may be recorded at the teacher's option.

Laboratories are generally wired so that several different master tapes can be running simultaneously. Individual booths or blocks of booths may thus receive a program in German, while another is hearing French. This flexibility is essential, as it allows segments of a class to work on different things; for example, a group of excellent students can work on a more advanced drill while the rest are using the regular drill.

Monitoring is the term used to indicate that the teacher is listening in. The console usually contains a switchboard more or less like a telephone switchboard. The teacher can switch to an individual student to check his progress, make suggestions and corrections, and give a grade. Two-way teacher-student communication is provided. If the teacher says nothing, the monitoring is done without the student's knowing just when his work is being checked. This furnishes an incentive to the student to make a good effort at all times, and gives the teacher a better idea of the student's average proficiency.

In the usual classroom situation the teacher is, in effect, monitoring and correcting one student, while the *rest* are silent. In the laboratory *all* the students are actively working during the monitoring of an individual.

B. Library Mode. The laboratory equipped for operation in the library mode can do everything the broadcast type can do. In addition there is a tape recorder (or the remotely controlled equivalent thereof) at each booth position. The drills, instead of being broadcast, are pre-recorded on *student tapes,* using the duplicating facilities built into the laboratory. Usually the student copies are prepared by placing a blank tape on every student machine while the laboratory is empty, starting all of them together by remote control, and broadcasting the master tape from the console. The broadcast is recorded on the master edge of each student tape, and is not thereafter erasable by the students.

When a class arrives for its laboratory work, each student is issued a pre-recorded student tape. In universities, students may arrive as individuals for study and take the correct tape from the shelves. Whether acting as a part of a class or as an individual, the student goes to a booth, loads the tape on the machine, and begins work. As students hear the master track, they record their own responses automatically on the same tape (the *student* track). They are free to stop the tape at any moment, backtrack, compare their responses with the correct answers in the anticipation drill, and make a new attempt. They automatically erase their old responses as new ones are recorded, but at no time can they erase the pre-recorded master track. The drill remains on the tape until the teacher withdraws the tape and has it erased on the bulk eraser.

The great advantage of the library mode is that students can work and rework drills at their own speed, according to their abilities. They can go over and over a difficult section until they become proficient—a thing that is impossible to do in the broadcast mode. There, if the student does not catch a word, he is in the same situation as a person who is in a movie and has missed the punch line of a joke: he must sit through the whole show again until that line comes up again. In the library mode, the student simply stops the show and backs it up whenever the need arises. High school laboratories so equipped will be at a great advantage, because the native abilities of the students are so wide-ranging.

The library system is also particularly needed in the university level, where the laboratory corresponds roughly to the library proper as a place for doing homework. Students arrive as individuals rather than as a group—this is actually the only difference between a high school and a university operation in most cases—and they draw the assigned tape, work, and leave individually.

C. Combinations. Some laboratories are predominantly of the broadcast type, with *a few* booths having individual tape machines. Such a laboratory will accommodate a class (using the broadcast facilities) plus some students from other classes working independently at the fully equipped library-type booths. Such a laboratory is quite effective as well as relatively economical, provided that self-correcting (anticipation) drills comprise most of the instructional material. It is most practical in situations where language classes use the laboratory as a class group, all receiving the same broadcast material simultaneously. The teacher has the same advantage as in the classroom for monitoring any student at any time, with the added advantage that while one student is monitored, all the *other* students are hard at work.

The fully equipped booths (those with tape decks for individual or group use) can be used as part of the regular laboratory class operation, or they may be used independently. If a class does not entirely fill the laboratory, the booths with tape decks may be left free for students from other courses to do homework, back work, or advanced study; or they may be assigned to members of the class who are more advanced or more retarded than the rest. These exceptional students may then work with prerecorded tapes; they can work at their own speed, stopping and backtracking at will. Slow students will profit from this facility particularly. Fast students may be given tapes in order to do more advanced or collateral work, while the remainder of the class does the current work.

Some combination laboratories have been modified to include a simple one-track recording instrument (disk or tape deck) for each ordinary booth, allowing the student to make a record of the broadcast and his own responses. He can then hear what he has done for self-criticism. The disadvantage of this is that he cannot erase his own efforts without also erasing the master track. So long as this simple instrument is of a single-track recording type, the student will not profit greatly, for all he can do is to listen to a record of [say] twenty minutes of imperfect or incorrect answers—his first attempt. His time would be better spent on a fresh try, because he is already aware of his errors through the mechanism of the four-phase anticipation drill. Here the advantage of the dual-track (or equivalent) individual recorder becomes clear: the class enters the fully equipped laboratory, hears and records the program of the first half of the period, working on the broadcast system. At this point each student has a dual-track student tape, and can then work independently during the second half of the period. He can hear his original mistakes, or he can begin afresh using only his recording of the broadcast master.

In summary, the fully equipped laboratory can be used for *every* kind of work, from simple broadcast teaching where the class works as a group, to totally independent and individual work. The combination of some fully equipped booths with a much larger number of broadcast booths of lesser flexibility will serve economically. The students in the simple microphone-headphone booth will generally learn just as well as those in a booth having recording facilities, if the proper drill techniques are used. Still, some fully equipped booths must be available in every laboratory for the student needing to go more slowly, for the excellent student in need of more challenging material, and for students using the laboratory for preparation of other courses. The latter students can be present in the laboratory, since they will in no way interfere with the conduct of a class in laboratory session.

D. Selection of Equipment. Inspect and carefully read specifications for the various makes and types of equipment available to see what each will do, how it looks, how well it will stand up under continuous use, and whether parts likely to wear out quickly (drive belts, for example) are easy to replace. Then, since a budget may govern, find out how much equipment costs, how many units you can afford under the circumstances, and whether it will fit in the space you have. The primary consideration is whether it will do all the things you want it to. Library-type equipment will do everything, and can simulate a broadcast laboratory; on the other hand, a broadcast laboratory can never simulate a library laboratory. The less versatile equipment cannot usually be later converted to *more* versatile equipment; you might have to make a fresh and expensive start later to get the versatility you need.

Do not hesitate to ask the manufacturers of laboratory equipment to demonstrate their materials. Insist on being permitted to test sample equipment over a period of several days without the presence of a glib salesman; see if you can operate it, and give it a thorough tryout. Names of manufacturers and the descriptions of their latest products are found in the advertisements of the *French Review*, the *Modern Language Journal*, *PMLA*, and similar professional language journals.

When you have narrowed the choice to a particular brand, most manufacturers will give you free planning and engineering advice. They will submit, for your approval and criticism, layouts for the positioning and wiring of your laboratory equipment. In this part of the planning they will be of real assistance.

16. Space for the Laboratory. A room or rooms for the housing of the laboratory equipment is necessary. If a room is arbitrarily assigned by authorities, the number of booths (maximum) is predetermined without regard to actual needs. Space should be assigned with regard to the needs of the language enrollment. If a whole class is to use the laboratory at a time, it is obvious that there must be as many booths in the laboratory as there are students in the largest language class. Any smaller number of booths will deprive some students of the instructional advantage to which they are entitled.

If the library system is to be used, a rough estimate of the number of booths needed can be obtained by dividing the total language enrollment by the number of laboratory periods per day. Thus if there were 586 students enrolled in all languages, and we arranged seven laboratory periods (of 40 minutes each) per day, we would compute

$$\frac{\text{enrollment}}{\text{lab. periods}} = \frac{586}{7} = 84 \text{ booths needed}$$

This computation assumes that every student will spend one period per day in the laboratory. If 84 booths are financially out of the question (this size might require two laboratory rooms), the number needed could be cut in two by (1) halving the length of the period, thus creating 14 periods per day, or (2) requiring laboratory attendance every *other* day. Further economies can be effected by extending the laboratory day (from 7 to 10 periods per day, for example, would reduce the booths needed to 59) or by other scheduling manipulations.

Assume that continuity of work is necessary: every student should work in the laboratory every day. Assume that long contact is necessary: try for an hour a day, and reduce this reluctantly. Strive to find the compromise (if necessary) least damaging to these factors.

A. The Laboratory Proper. The space for the student booths can be computed roughly as follows: each booth needs a floor space of about $3\frac{1}{2}$ feet wide by 6 feet deep, allowing adequate room for chair and passage space. This is 21 square feet per booth for a comfortably roomy laboratory. If you planned to install a 30-booth laboratory, the space needed for the student portion would be 630 square feet. Allow additional space for side aisles and (if it is to go in the main laboratory) the console and controls, book pigeonholes, entrance space, room for doors to swing, and cabinets. Provide a soundproof projection booth or platform at the rear of the laboratory for projecting slides, filmstrips, and films. This space must have audio and electric outlets and remote controls if possible. A projection screen is located high at the front of the laboratory, with a clear view above booth fronts. Provide for coupling the projector into a student audio channel.

B. The Recording Studio. Absolutely necessary is a separate room for making the master recordings. This room may be small, perhaps 8 x 10 feet in size, and could be erected within the larger room. It must be soundproofed by acoustical tile treatment, wall insulation, cork floor, and treated door. There must be a double-glazed window (two different thicknesses of glass, installed at a slight angle to each other, rather than exactly parallel), and the room should be air-conditioned with a silent system. Ventilation is most important.

This room is exclusively for making recordings. It will be free of extraneous noises—passing trucks, playground shouts, slamming doors, and the like. Master tapes and blank master tapes may be kept there on shelves installed for the purpose. Sufficient electrical outlets for recorder, lights, and accessories are needed. Audio channels (both in and out) should have terminals here, too. A permanent table for the instruments may be constructed along one wall.

C. Storage Room. An additional room of the same dimensions as the recording studio should be provided, with access to the laboratory. This room is for the storage of blank tapes, recorded tapes, spare parts, and other supplies. It should be provided with ample shelves, and with a workbench for assistants to use for splicing tapes, repairing machinery, erasing tapes on the bulk eraser, making copies of tapes, and the like. It should be well lighted and well ventilated.

D. Control Room. If the monitoring console is not located in the laboratory proper (its usual place), a room similar in construction to the recording studio might serve as a control room. It would also be an office for the laboratory director, and a place for storing scripts and administrative records. Public school regulations often require the physical presence of a teacher in the same room with the students, so the teacher's console must then be located in the laboratory proper.

17. Installation and Construction Details. After space has been allocated, mark the exact position of partitions (for recording studio, storage room), rows of booths, console, and other furniture on the floor with chalk. This will serve you as a guide in determining adequate lighting, and will enable the electricians to determine the routes for electrical and audio wiring.

A. Sequence of Construction. (1) Have necessary partitions installed, doors hung, and other building construction done; (2) Any new electrical circuits, including the installation of overhead lights, new 110-volt outlets, junction boxes, master control switch, and the like; (3) Air-conditioning or other ventilating system; (4) Acoustical tile and soundproofing; (5)

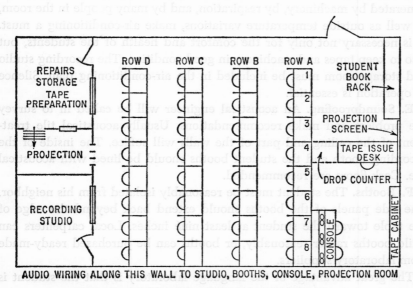

AUDIO WIRING ALONG THIS WALL TO STUDIO, BOOTHS, CONSOLE, PROJECTION ROOM

Fig. 5: A 32-Position Language Laboratory

Installation and fastening of booths, permanent cabinets, etc.; (6) Painting and finishing; (7) The equipment manufacturer or dealer installs the equipment selected, including audio wiring; (8) Chairs and other supplementary furniture and equipment are moved in.

B. Building Work. Carpenters are given the floor plan and construction specifications for building the soundproof recording studio. They build the necessary rooms and other construction. Some electrical work needs to be done before walls are finished, so the electrical contractor needs to be contacted at this time.

C. Electrical. The electrical contractor will install power circuits to operate machinery. He must know the location of the equipment and the current drawn by each machine. Get the figures from the manufacturers. Include the air-conditioning and ventilators, and provide floor outlets even where there is no immediate need—they will come in handy. The floor plan and the chalk lines on the floor will help place the overhead lights.

A master switch should control *all* circuits except lights. This switch should be near the monitoring console. It is a safeguard that all machines have been turned off. The master switch should have a pilot light.

D. Ventilation. Air-conditioning is essential for the laboratory. Heat generated by machinery, by respiration, and by many people in the room, as well as outside temperature variations, make air-conditioning a must. It is necessary not only for the comfort and health of the students, but also to keep tapes and machinery in good condition. The recording studio and storage room must be included in the air-conditioning plan. Silence of operation is essential.

E. Soundproofing. An acoustical engineer will be called in to survey the problem and make recommendations. Usually acoustical tile treatment of the ceiling and part of the walls will suffice. The inside of the recording booth and the student booths should be lined with acoustical tile. Cork floors are recommended.

F. Booths. The student must be reasonably isolated from his neighbor. The side panels of the booths should extend back beyond the edge of the table toward the student at least nine inches. Local carpenters can build booths rather reasonably, or booths can be purchased ready-made from laboratory suppliers.

The great advantage of the language laboratory is that the student is freed from embarrassment and inhibitions often present in the classroom. He knows that the mechanical "teacher"—the tape—is infinitely patient, that there will be no evidence of amusement at his expense when he blunders, and that he can achieve a degree of excellence in the laboratory that will make the forthcoming classroom recitation a pleasure. Audio privacy at this crucial point of instruction (in the laboratory) is provided by the earphones and the closed electrical circuit. At the same time the high partitions of the front and sides provide visual isolation and the illusion of being alone. This priceless simulation of complete privacy during a process requiring intense concentration should not be destroyed in any way. For this reason it is inadvisable to have transparent panels in the front of the booth, or to destroy visual privacy in any other way. The projection of visual aids should be high enough above the booth tops in any case so that vision is clear from all angles. Since booth sides will block vision of students in lateral positions in the laboratory anyway, transparent fronts merely destroy visual privacy without contributing to improved visual aid presentation.

G. **Audio Wiring.** When booths have been placed, audio wiring (connecting console, booths, recording studio, and projection booth) should

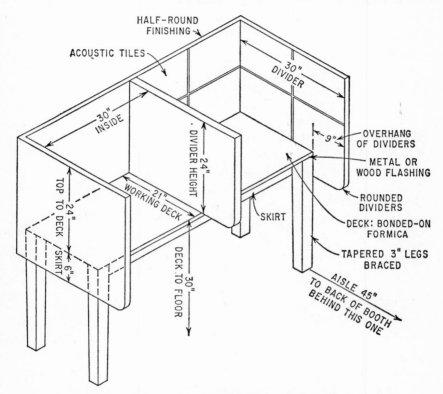

Fig. 6: Design for a Booth Unit of Two Places

be done by the supplier of the laboratory equipment. It should be agreed at the time of contracting for the installation that he will handle this matter.

H. **Safety Regulations.** Compliance with local fire regulations must be ascertained in the planning stage (often laboratory booths must be fastened permanently to the floor when wiring is to be installed). Wiring must meet the electrical code requirements. Adequate exits, doors opening outward, fire extinguishers, and other such matters must be attended to.

I. Protection of Equipment. Adequate locks and a plan for control of keys are needed. Get insurance on the laboratory and equipment, and liability insurance. If the school coverage in existence does not extend to the laboratory, a special policy should be purchased.

Fig. 6: Design for a Booth Unit of Two Places

be done by the supplies of the laboratory equipment. It should be agreed at the time of contracting for the installation that he will handle this matter.

H. Safety Regulations. Compliance with local fire regulations must be ascertained in the planning stage (often laboratory booths must be fastened permanently to the floor when wiring is to be installed.). Wiring must meet the electrical code requirements. Adequate exits, doors open-

Tape Library and Student Routine

WE SHALL now examine the problems of producing and managing drill material in its recorded form, and of establishing a student routine in the language laboratory. Regardless of the physical nature of the laboratory, there must be a stock of recorded materials in tape or disk form. In as much as magnetic tapes are standard, we shall refer to such recorded materials as tapes, with the understanding that the same principles apply to other forms of recordings. The essential function of the laboratory is to transmit the *sound* to the student so that he can hear it clearly and respond to the stimuli.

18. Masters. Tapes on which the material of the tapescripts is originally recorded are called *master* tapes. Masters should be produced on fine recording instruments, such as the Ampex, Sony, Concertone, or Magnecord. One such instrument should be designated as the master recorder and kept in the recording studio for the use of teachers. Master tapes are usually made at the speed of 7½ inches per second (i.p.s.) for highest fidelity in the process of broadcasting to student positions. The slow speed (3¾ i.p.s.) is usually adequate for human speech, but is not recommended for laboratory masters. It is recommended that a master not exceed 15 to 20 minutes in length, because the student should repeat the drill twice during a given laboratory period, and because the normal span of attention is strained on longer, unrelieved drills.

The most convenient size reel for use as a master tape is the 5-inch reel of tape. This reel will hold a full 20-minute master (or a shorter drill, of course). Handling of masters is much easier if each drill is on a separate tape than if several drills are strung together on a longer tape. In the latter case, identification of a specific drill is more difficult; and the savings in tape are not significant.

A. Identification of Masters. Before a drill can be recorded, the tape number must be determined so that it can be spoken at the start of the tape. This number, taken from the *tape register book* (Fig. 9, § 26B), is written on the script at beginning and end for the appropriate announcement. As soon as a recording is completed, the teacher marks the word "Master" and the tape number on the white leader tape with a ball-point pen. The reel itself is marked by placing the tape number on a self-adhesive label, which is in turn attached to the plastic reel on the side visible when the reel is on the playback machines. A similar label is placed on the shelfback of the box in a uniform location.

A **duplicate master** should be made in broadcast-type laboratories. This is the copy used by the technicians for actual transmissions. If it breaks or is damaged, the master can be substituted at once as an emergency measure, and the laboratory routine will not be interrupted. If no duplicate is made and the master is seriously damaged, a great deal of trouble results: the script must be found and the entire recording process repeated—all because a duplicate master was not dubbed.

B. Labeling and Shelving. Labels recommended are self-adhesive labels measuring ⅜ x 1¼ inches, available in sheets in most stationery stores. Rubber stamps having bands of numbers can be used for a neat numbering job. (Specific brands are recommended in Sections 27D and G.)

Tapes are shelved according to language, and within the language by course. Within a course the tapes are shelved serially according to the number following the dash. (A numbering system is suggested in Section 20.)

C. Circulation. Master tapes are not circulated to the students. Only teachers and technicians have access to them. If a technician is responsible for playing the tape, the teacher should furnish a schedule of tapes to be played each period, showing tape numbers, channels to be used, and starting times.

D. Storage. Master tapes are accumulated as courses progress, so that the second year the teachers will not have so heavy a load of drill construction and recording as the first. A complete card catalogue is maintained as teachers must be able to find the drills they need quickly. When a new textbook replaces an old one, a committee should survey the drills used with the old text to see whether the masters should be erased and returned to the stock of available blank tapes. Some will be worth retaining. Others, too closely associated with the old text, should be returned to blank stock. This process we may term *retirement of tapes*. Since the tapes are completely erasable and reusable, a considerable investment in tapes is kept active in this way.

E. Commercial and Publishers' Tapes. There are many good commercially available tapes for use with language courses. If student copies are to be made, the written permission of the manufacturer should be secured. If the manufacturer is assured that the copies will not be sold or removed from the laboratory, this permission is usually forthcoming.

Many publishers now have recordings—both tape and disk—of drills and exercises associated with their textbooks. Several publishers, such as the Oxford University Press, will lend their master tapes for copying to schools that have adopted their textbooks. In adopting a textbook, consider the availability of such tapes, free of charge. The service will save the faculty hundreds of hours of work. (See *Materials List,* New York: MLA, 1959. Price 50 cents.)

19. Student Tapes. Laboratories operating on the library system in whole or in part must produce, label, shelve, and distribute student copies. The term used for making such copies is *dubbing.* Mylar tape (1 mil) is recommended for its strength. Five-inch reels are purchased and split into two student reels. Half of the tape is run off onto an empty 5-inch reel, thus creating two standard student tapes of 20-minute duration * at slow speed (3¾ i.p.s.). A length of white leader is spliced on the front of each tape to protect the loose end.

A. Dubbing—Production of Multiple Student Copies. Laboratories operating on the library system must have a means of producing multiple copies of the master tape quickly and easily. The simplest arrangement is for each student tape deck to be a duplicating machine, on which a blank tape can be loaded for dubbing on the master track only. The instructor should have control of the starting and stopping of the tape movements and of the volume and sound quality at the console. With this arrangement a teacher can start a number of machines all together, broadcast the drill from a master to the master track of each student tape, stop the machines, collect, label, and shelve the copies. All dubbing operations are controlled from the monitoring console.

This process can be done when the laboratory is not in use, or can be accomplished even as the students are hearing the broadcast associated

* A full 5-inch reel of 1-mil Mylar tape may actually run as long as 40 to 42 minutes, so that when split into two student tapes, the standard length would be about 20 minutes at slow speed. When the supply of tapes actually being used arrives, the best procedure is to time the full reel, and split them according to elapsed time.

with the recording process. The equipment of manufacturers is varied, and new types of remote control systems are being introduced rapidly.

B. Labeling and Shelving. Student copies are labeled with the same number as the master (minus the suffix M). The number is placed only on the box. Rapid retirement of student tapes makes it inadvisable to label the reels and leaders. The same type of label is used as for master tapes.

As in a library, tapes may be shelved under the "open stack" system for mature students, or "closed stack" for less mature ones. Under the latter system the teacher or an assistant issues the tapes and receives them back. In each case, for rapid location, the tapes are shelved according to language, course, and serial number. The same precautions taken by a library to safeguard its reference books should be taken in the language laboratory to control student tapes.

C. Quantities Needed. A decision as to how many student tapes to have available depends upon the way the laboratory operates. In elementary and high school laboratories, a complete class uses the laboratory at one time, and there must be sufficient copies to accommodate the largest class in a given course. One copy for each booth would be the maximum useful number, of course.

In universities where the students may be required to attend the laboratory, *but at random times* that fit their diverse schedules, a tabulation by course and hour is made during registration (see Fig. 12). In this way the laboratory knows how many French 1 students are supposed to attend the laboratory at 9 a.m., for example, how many at 10:00, and so on. The hour having the largest number of French 1 students might be 11:00 with 34 expected. This would set the maximum number of French 1 library tapes needed at 34.

If attendance is random—not specifically controlled by scheduling—an estimate is made using the percentages of enrollment in various courses. The first few days will let the attendants know if they are running short of copies. It is usually a practical procedure to provide an intentionally overlarge supply of student tapes during the first week of operation. The number of unused tapes is noted so that thereafter duplication of tapes may be based on actual needs.

D. Retirement of Student Tapes. The current lesson of any course is represented by a full strength of student tapes—enough to meet the maximum possible demand. As soon as a lesson becomes an old lesson, all the student tapes for that lesson are retired except about 10 per cent.

The retired tapes are simply removed from the shelf, erased on a bulk eraser, and returned to blank student tape stock for use on more advanced lessons. The labels are pulled off when the tape is erased.

The remaining 10 per cent (or a minimum of two copies) is left on the shelf for review purposes for the rest of the semester.

This system effects an important economy with regard to student tapes. Suppose it were standard practice to make 34 student copies for French 1. Compare the tapes on the shelf under two systems—one in which every lesson is retained at full strength, and one in which the retirement system is used:

LESSON	TAPES ON SHELF	
	FULL STRENGTH	RETIREMENT SYSTEM
6. (current)	34	34
5. (old)	34	3 (review)
4. (old)	34	3 (review)
3. (old)	34	3 (review)
2. (old)	34	3 (review)
1. (old)	34	3 (review)
TOTAL TAPES ON SHELF	204	49

(*after 6 lessons*)

Under the tape retirement system, 31 tapes were withdrawn, erased, and returned to stock as each lesson became non-current.

On the other hand, if there are plenty of tapes, retention of back lessons in full strength will sharply reduce the job of dubbing for the following year's work. If the same book is to be used, and tapes are plentiful, keep the tapes in storage for use the next time the course is given. When the retirement system is used, the saving in tapes is made at the expense of time and labor necessary to dub new copies. As long as the master is retained, with remote control equipment this is a small matter.

E. Accommodation Dubbing. Often students who have tape recorders at home request copies of the drills for home study. If assistants in the laboratory have time for it, the copying is often done free of charge, using the student's own tape. The student's interest in the language justifies the small expenditure of time needed to make the copy.

20. Numbering System. Numbers assigned to tapes should convey some information about the tapes by indicating at least the language and course. The full number is spoken at the beginning and end of every tape and marked on the box label.

A simple system is to use first a letter designating the language ($F =$ French, $G =$ German, $I =$ Italian, $R =$ Russian, $S =$ Spanish, etc.); next a number designating the semester or course number; a dash; a number indicating the serial or lesson:

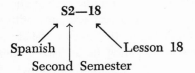

$$S2-18$$

Spanish   Lesson 18

Second Semester

If identification by year is also useful, the year can be prefixed: **60 S2-18** is a tape number that tells us that the tape is one made in 1960, that it is second-semester Spanish, and is number 18 of a series, *or* Lesson 18 in the text used that year. Master tapes have the suffix M to distinguish them from student tapes: **60 S2-18M** would be the master from which the student tape was made.

Information as to the exact *text reference*, grammatical *content*, and running *time* in minutes is recorded in two places: on the master box, and in the tape register book (Fig. 9). This information is recorded the moment the master tape is completed. It is later transcribed to the card catalogue.

Blocks of numbers may be reserved to indicate special uses:

-01 through -199	Basic Course Materials
-200 through -499	Cultural, Literary, Musical
-500 through -599	Tests, Examinations, Practice Tests

Thus if you picked up a tape bearing the number G3-251, you would know without reference to the tape register that it was a third-semester German tape of a cultural nature, not directly related to the textbook. Using this system, the number before the dash indicates the language and level, and the number after the dash shows the type of material contained on the tape, as well as the serial. When the number blocks for a particular laboratory have been established, it is helpful to make a large poster showing them so that students and teachers may conveniently refer to these categories.

21. Card Catalogue. A card catalogue with complete information pertaining to recorded material available in the laboratory should be maintained. This catalogue should include material on disks and tapes, and filmstrip material. Because of the nature of language instruction, a separate catalogue is kept for each language; the separation may be done by having a separate file drawer for each language, or by using differently colored cards for the various languages.

Headings for the cards are cross-referenced as completely as possible. Care should be taken to list a grammatical subject under all the usual or possible terminologies. In French, for example, the *passé composé* is also known as the *past indefinite* and *compound past*. One of these is selected as standard, and a cross-reference card (e.g. "Past Indefinite: see *passé composé*") is placed in the catalogue at each alphabetical location for other terms of identical meaning.

Cards should be made and placed in the catalogue for each **grammatical subject** (e.g. *direct object pronouns, agreement of adjectives, use of dative case, regular -er verbs,* etc.); for **cultural subjects** (e.g. the *Louvre, Madrid, Uffizi Gallery, Châteaux of the Loire,* interview with *Camus, Babar*) taken from prerecorded material, recorded magazines such as the French *Sonorama,* or disks; and finally by **textbook** and page. For textbook cards, the author's name is the location criterion: all page reference cards to his textbook are grouped numerically after his name and title of the text.

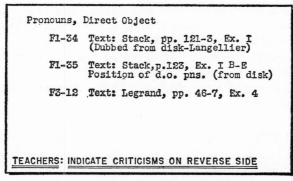

Fig. 7: Subject Card in the Catalogue

A sample layout for a grammatical subject card is shown in Fig. 7. The necessary information contained thereon, in order, is:

1. Grammatical or structural title.
2. Tape numbers listed in order of increasing level.
3. Textbook reference, page numbers and exercise numbers for each tape listed.
4. Space for teachers' criticism (usually on reverse side).

The card for cultural subjects lists similar information, except that the textbook reference is absent, and more information about the nature of the recording is shown:

1. Title of material (e.g. *Fables of La Fontaine*). A cross-reference under La Fontaine is needed.
2. Tape number (if on tape) or record number. Disk records acquired must be shelved; a convenient way is to assign a number from the tape register as for tapes, adding the suffix *D* (disk): F5-305D. Disks are stored in numerical order, just like tapes.
3. Description of material (names of fables on this disk).
4. Manufacturer's number, source, and cost.

The textbook card lists the following information, in order:

1. Last name (and, if needed for identification, first name and middle initial) of author.
2. Name or abbreviation of textbook. When abbreviations are used, place a card at the beginning of each tray listing the abbreviations.
3. Page numbers of taped material in a box in the upper right-hand corner for quick reference. Under a given author's book, it is this entry that governs the order of cards.
4. Grammatical or structural title of material covered.
5. Exercise numbers.
6. Numbers of tapes dealing with the specific pages shown on the card.

22. Student Orientation. Students should be thoroughly oriented to the use of the laboratory at the beginning of the semester. Good training at that point will make the laboratory operate smoothly and efficiently. Orientation is of two types: *mechanical* and *linguistic*. Mechanical orientation pertains to the actions of the student upon entering the laboratory —getting tape, finding a place, adjusting the headsets and microphone, and manipulating the equipment. Linguistic orientation means teaching the student how an anticipation pattern drill works.

Finally, the student must be taught how to "close station." Turning off the machinery, hanging up the headset, clearing off the deck, putting the chair in position, and (if applicable) returning the tape to its proper position are all matters of training.

A. Pre-laboratory Orientation. The teacher explains the purpose of the laboratory, scheduling, and attendance rules. He describes the routine. He tells the students what they are expected to do the very first time they enter the laboratory. If available, an orientation movie is shown so

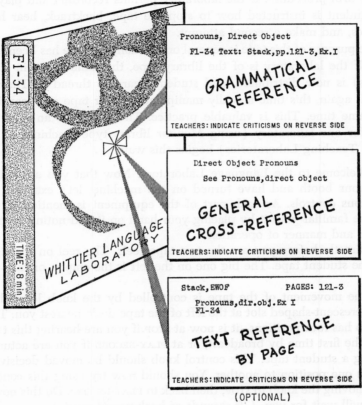

Fig. 8: Cards Needed for a Tape Card Catalogue

that the students will see a laboratory in action before they actually visit one.*

B. Orientation Tape. The students enter the laboratory where they are assigned their positions in the booths. The surroundings and equipment will be strange to them, so they are guided rather carefully. A specially prepared orientation tape is broadcast to all of them. This tape is designed to give both mechanical and linguistic orientation. First it

---

* Such a film (for library laboratory) is *New Dimensions in Language Teaching*, distributed by the Rarig Motion Picture Co., Seattle, Washington.

explains each part of the equipment and control mechanism in simple terms and logical order, and the students handle each part as it is mentioned.

Next some sample drills are presented in English to orient the student to the drill procedure. If the laboratory permits recording and playback, the student is instructed how to stop the tape, backtrack, hear his responses, and make a second attempt.

The purpose of this tape is general orientation; the tape has been *broadcast*. If the laboratory is of the library type, the same tape (in student copies) is now distributed, and students learn to thread it. They then hear it again, this time actually manipulating their tape and learning at the same time. This is valuable practice. The script for an orientation tape for one laboratory (using *Monitor* library-type machines of Electronic Teaching Laboratories) begins this way:

> Welcome to the Language Laboratory. Now that you are seated at your booth and have turned on the machine, let's examine the various controls. As each part of the equipment is mentioned, become familiar with it by placing your hand on it and noting its purpose and manner of operation.
>
> Directly before you are the two tape reels. The reel on the right is the student tape. The big one on the left is the empty, or take-up, reel.
>
> The movement of the tape is controlled by the knob located in the crescent-shaped slot at the left of the tape deck, nearest you. This knob has four positions—it is now at STOP if you are hearing this tape for the first time by broadcast, or at PLAY-RECORD if you are actually using a student tape. This control knob should be moved decisively from one position to another. You should now try using this control by moving the knob to STOP, then back to PLAY-RECORD. Do this now— we will wait for you. (*10 seconds of background music*)
>
> Now that the tape is moving again, notice the other two positions for the control knob. These positions at the extreme ends of the slot are the fast forward and fast rewind positions. . . . (etc.)
>
> Now observe the vertical panel on the right. It contains two control knobs and, at the top, a meter. The knob nearer you is the on-off switch and volume control, and works just like the volume control on your radio at home. . . . (etc.)

The orientation tape continues along these lines to give the student a full acquaintance with the parts of the tape mechanism and all other controls and equipment at the student position. Instructions can be included on how things should be left upon closing station. The mechanical orientation being concluded, the narration on the tape turns to teaching the student how the anticipation drills work so that the routine of use will be quite clear:

. . . Now that we have examined all the controls, let's see how the tape drills are organized. Set your function control [by now identified] to LISTEN-RECORD—remember, this is the knob directly under the meter on the right-hand vertical panel (*pause*). Be sure the microphone is plugged in. You are now ready to record.

This drill is called an anticipation drill. You will hear a short sentence, like "I'm working." Since the purpose of this particular sample drill is to make the sentence negative, you then say, "I'm not working." Then you will hear the correct answer for comparison, and you should repeat the correct answer. Join in as soon as you understand.

Anticipation Drill, Negation of English Verbs.

1. I'm working. # (SIMULATED STUDENT VOICE: *I'm not working.*)
   I'm not working. # (SIMULATED STUDENT VOICE: *I'm not working.*)

2. I'm talking. # (STUDENT VOICE: *I'm not talking.*)
   I'm not talking. # (STUDENT VOICE: *I'm not talking.*)

3. John's thinking. #
   John's not thinking. #

4. We're painting. #
   We're not painting. #

5. You're leaving. #
   You're not leaving. #

End of sample anticipation drill.

Now you will be able to hear how well you have done this drill. Turn the function knob to PLAYBACK. Remember, this is the knob directly under the meter. Turn it clockwise one click (*pause*). As soon as you receive the signal, you will stop the tape with the movement control, rewind it just a moment by putting the knob in the fast rewind position to the extreme right of the crescent-shaped slot, and stop the tape. Then move the knob to PLAY-RECORD again to hear what you have done. Do this now.

(10 seconds of background music)

If you think you could do better, do this drill again. To record a new attempt, turn the *function* control back to LISTEN-RECORD position, that is, one click counter-clockwise. Rewind the tape for just a moment to the beginning of the drill, and repeat the drill a second time. Your first answers will automatically be erased, and your new ones will be recorded.

Continue using the tape this way for practice. If you have any difficulty or questions, raise your hand. When the lights in the laboratory blink, rewind your tape completely, put the reel of tape in the storage box, and wait for further instructions.

We hope that you will find working in the laboratory both profitable and enjoyable.

The use of this kind of orientation tape permits the student to get supervised practice at the very same time as he is receiving basic instruction in narration form.

23. Laboratory Routine. Train the students to follow a certain desirable routine in the laboratory. This routine includes leaving books and other impedimenta in the book pigeonholes that should be provided near the entrance to the laboratory, and especially the replacement of earphones, chairs, and tapes in precisely the prescribed positions. The student should be made to feel his responsibility to the next user of the laboratory. If he replaces a tape so that the label is not showing, or leaves the earphones in a tangle, the next student is unnecessarily inconvenienced.

Students will soon fall into desirable habits in their laboratory routine if they are informed at the outset of the standard ways of doing things. They should then be closely observed during the first few laboratory periods. Every time a student leaves his booth an assistant should check to see that the machine is turned off and the equipment in proper order; when a student replaces a tape on the shelf, its position should be verified. Many students are careless or thoughtless, but if it is pointed out to them what they have done incorrectly, they soon learn to perform as expected. This close surveillance at the beginning of the laboratory operation can be relaxed considerably after it is observed that most students habitually follow the standard routine.

24. Laboratory Assignments. Every assignment should include the number of the tape; the student is expected to use the number as part of his studies. In colleges and universities the assignment (whether given orally or on an assignment sheet) is a reference to a textbook or other material to be read before coming to class. The tape number given is likewise material to be studied as part of advance preparation. The language student should arrive in class prepared: he should have oral and aural mastery of the recorded lesson assigned. Language laboratories in universities using the library system serve the same purpose with regard to the spoken language as regular libraries do with regard to the body of written language. The laboratory is the place to prepare the language lesson, just as the library is the place to prepare a history lesson. Tapes are shelved by subject and number in the laboratory, just as books are shelved by the Dewey Decimal System in the library. If the student knows the number of the assigned book or tape, he can get it from the shelves and work at his own best speed.

High school laboratories and other laboratories using the broadcast system will have to set up schedules for tape broadcasts. Usually a class will enter the laboratory as a unit, and the teacher will select and broadcast the correct tape. Even so, it is well to inform the students of the tape number associated with each textbook lesson, and have them mark the number on the appropriate page. Then when they wish to review during a study period they may request a tape by number. If a combination library-broadcast laboratory is used, the student may be issued a student copy of the tape for study and review at one of the library-type booths having an individual tape deck.

Laboratory Administration

ALTHOUGH the teacher's task of constructing effective drills is formidable enough, it is not the end of the trail. There remains the problem of physical maintenance of equipment and facilities, the necessity of close scheduling, the need for carrying out daily mechanical tasks such as tape erasure, splicing, checking switches, and the like. In this chapter we shall examine the distribution of routine duties among the personnel, the use of administrative forms, the scheduling of machine use and of student attendance, and the acquisition of stocks and supplies for the laboratory.

25. **Personnel.** The faculty of the language department, student assistants, and contract maintenance personnel comprise the operating group for most laboratories. The main responsibility lies, of course, with the faculty. The faculty members train the student assistants, and call in expert electronics help when needed. Ordinarily the department chairman is responsible for the installation and operation of the laboratory, and he does this in close co-ordination with his administrative superiors. Once the laboratory is in steady operation as a part of the departmental organization, one faculty member is usually appointed as director of the language laboratory. This assignment should be counter-balanced by a reduction of the teaching load for the person serving as director. Duty as director might well be rotated annually, for two reasons: (1) it provides the incumbent with excellent experience in laboratory administration; and (2) it makes for more equitable sharing of this non-teaching duty.

The principal duties in any laboratory are indicated below according to the persons who would perform them under normal circumstances:

A. Director. The director is a member of the teaching staff designated to assume administrative responsibility for the physical operation of the language laboratory. He schedules the use of equipment, selects and trains student assistants, maintains stocks of supplies, maintains all equipment in good order (using assistants or outside technicians), and safe-guards the contents of the laboratory. His function is one of scheduling, co-ordination, and supervision.

If the position of director is rotated, the teacher due to assume the duties next should serve as deputy director, at least during the last month or two of the academic year. This will be on-the-job training for the following year.

B. Faculty. The language teachers are responsible for preparing and recording laboratory drills, registering the numbers of the master tapes they have made in the register book, and indicating to the student assist-ants how many copies are to be made. The teacher also indicates on the first page of the script (see Fig. 11) how the tape is to be listed in the card catalogue. The assistant charged with typing out the cards will use this information in making the cards for that particular tape. The teacher should *follow up this procedure by checking* to see that the tape copies have actually been made, labeled properly, and shelved; that the cards are in the card catalogue; that the script has been filed in the proper place in the filing cabinet reserved for scripts. Do not *assume* that it has been done or shift the responsibility to the director.

Much duplication of effort can be saved if teachers giving the same course will meet in committee to divide up the making of drills, each teacher to make drills for several lessons. If the standard drills outlined in Chapter II are used and patterns are set up in a consistent way, uni-formly good drills will then be available for all the material in the textbook.

At the first committee meeting the work is divided up. The limiting factors for each lesson are the grammatical content of the lesson, and the cumulative vocabulary to that point. The drills for a lesson are to teach just the grammatical point being discussed in the book at that moment, and must stay within the vocabulary range to that point.

At the second meeting the scripts for the first few lessons are sampled, discussed, improved where necessary, and approved. It is decided who will read the drills onto the tape, and a schedule is set up with the director for making the tapes. Numbers are assigned and entered in the tape register. These numbers are used in assignment sheets even though the tapes may not actually be available yet.

Further meetings are held as time goes on to examine and improve scripts for forthcoming lessons, and to set up further recording schedules, keeping ahead of the students' need for the drills.

A great aid to drill construction is a vocabulary notebook, listing words by parts of speech in the order they appear in the textbook. Thus the notebook would start with a page labeled "Lesson I," and under this heading would be several columns vertically arranged. There would be a column for *nouns, masculine,* one for *nouns, feminine,* one for *verbs, first conjugation,* one for *verbs, second conjugation; verbs, third conjugation; verbs, irregular; adverbs; prepositions; adjectives,* and so on. In patterning drills, this notebook will be invaluable. A teacher preparing a drill on verbs to accompany Lesson 12 (for example) can see at a glance all the verbs studied to that point, and all other vocabulary for which the students are responsible.

Teachers should inform the students of the tape numbers that correspond to each lesson, so that the student will be able to write this number in his notes. In library-type laboratories this will be part of his assignment; in broadcast-type laboratories he may wish to request the tape for special playing or review.

C. Student Assistants. Mature, serious students with special interest in languages or in mechanical devices such as tape recorders should be invited to try out for positions (sometimes unpaid, sometimes paid at regular student rates) as laboratory assistants. If they can be paid, the laboratory does not have to rely on good will alone to assure performance of necessary duties. The laboratory assistants assist other students in operating equipment, repair broken or tangled tape, make copies of master tapes as ordered in column 4 of the tape register (Fig. 9), erase tapes designated for retirement, and maintain the stock inventory. They also play tapes on the central monitoring console in some laboratories, following a posted schedule that indicates the tape numbers to be used, the time of the playing, and the booths to which each tape is to be broadcast. The director is charged with preparing this schedule and assigning assistants to duty hours.

Laboratory assistants check the tape register daily to see what tapes must be copied. If a master tape has been made (indicated by a checkmark in column 3), the assistant takes the master from the shelf and makes the number of copies indicated in column 4. After labeling and shelving the copies, he alters the inventory card to deduct the number of tapes used. He replaces the master and checks or initials column 5 of the tape register to show that the work is complete. Assistants should observe the second column (*Date Needed*) so that the copies needed first are made first, and so that student tapes are not made too far in advance, which would tie up tape stock that might be required for more immediate lessons.

Language laboratories in high schools and elementary schools may find a good source of reliable assistants in a near-by college or university. There are many serious college students interested in the operation of electronic equipment and in new language-teaching devices, who could be found by conferring with members of the faculty. The best information can be obtained by calling on the departments of language, education, and physics.

University departments of education might be quite amenable to allowing degree candidates to absolve a part of their certification requirements through practical experience in a language laboratory. Such work falls within the realm of audio-visual aids and practice teaching. Certainly any university student who is planning to teach languages (including English) should be quite familiar with the operational techniques of the laboratory. These techniques are simply a highly specialized application of audio-visual methods. The needs of a language teacher in this regard are not fully met by most existing required courses in audio-visual aids. If the director of a high school or elementary school language laboratory exploits this possibility by proposing an arrangement whereby university students receive credit for the work in the school laboratory, it seems likely that the suggestion would be welcomed by the university faculties. It is an arrangement of benefit both to the laboratory and the student; one receives much-needed assistance, and the other invaluable training. Such an apprenticeship system would contribute materially to the profession if it became generally established.

D. Technical Maintenance. There are two kinds of maintenance: preventive and remedial. Preventive maintenance entails the performance of periodic inspections and adjustments, including cleaning, replacement of worn or weak parts, and the like. This should be done on a regular schedule by trained personnel—often electronically talented students. Good preventive maintenance is far better than waiting for something to go wrong.

Serious or complicated trouble that cannot be remedied by laboratory personnel must be handled by skilled technicians. The school can, if very large and affluent, employ a full- or part-time skilled technician to handle repairs. In some laboratories repairs are made daily (but not hourly) in the laboratory repair room. If (as is likely to be the case) it is not feasible to have a regularly employed technician on the staff, the other main possibilities are (1) technical aid from the school electrical department or physics department on a regular basis, (2) service on a call-as-needed basis by the distributor of the equipment or by a local highly qualified repairman, or (3) service on a contract basis, including regular calls—perhaps weekly or more often as experience will dictate—by a local repairman. Small laboratories usually rely on one of the last two alternatives. If the equipment chosen for the laboratory is ruggedly constructed the maintenance problem will be small.

WARNING! Require the technician or contractor who installs the audio wiring of your laboratory to provide you with a complete wiring diagram, including color coding. Put this on file where it can be found quickly. If your regular dealer or technician goes out of business or is ill, or for some other reason a strange technician must find trouble, this diagram will save you much expense. Without it circuits must be traced—at a cost of several dollars per hour to you.

Also lay in a stock of spare parts—enough to build a complete machine of the type you are using—and a large supply of springs, flexible belts, washers and screws, knobs, and other parts susceptible to loss or wear. Ask your distributor to make up a kit of spare parts on this basis.

26. Administrative Forms and Records. The main forms that are useful in the language laboratory are (1) the card catalogue, already described in detail in § 21, (2) the tape register book, and (3) tape inventory. In addition there are various schedules needed—for student use under the library system, for use of the recording studio by teachers, for duty hours of laboratory assistants, for example.

A. Card Catalogue. This is a fully cross-referenced catalogue of available tapes, organized alphabetically and by languages (using a color coding). It enables teachers and students to find needed tapes quickly. (See § 21)

B. Tape Register Book. This is a book containing mimeographed or printed forms on which tape numbers are listed serially. Referring to Fig. 9, it will be noted that the page heading indicates the name of the language and the course (or number of the semester level). The block of numbers appearing on that page is shown in the upper right-hand corner.

Column 1 is the place where tape numbers are listed as they are planned for the course. This number is written on the script, and read as part of the tape format. When the use of the tape is correlated with the syllabus of the course and with the lesson plan, the date the tape will be needed is written in column 2. When the tape is made by the teacher a checkmark is placed in column 3. At the same time, the teacher writes the quantity of student copies to be made in column 4, so that assistants will prepare the proper number. When copies have been made, the assistant (or teacher) doing the work checks or initials column 5.

French					1		01-	

LANGUAGE — COURSE OR SEMESTER — BLOCK OF NUMBERS

F FRENCH
G GERMAN
R RUSSIAN
S SPANISH

01-199 BASIC
200-499 CULTURAL
500-599 TESTS

(1) TAPE NUMBER Assigned	(2) DATE Needed	(3) MASTER MADE ✓	(4) COPIES Needed	(5) Done ✓	(6) DESCRIPTION AND REFERENCE (Text)	RUNNING TIME (min)	(7) RESERVED: INITIALS
F1-01	9/20	✓	20	✓	Stack, p. 12, Ex A	14	LB
F1-02	9/24	✓	20	✓	Stack, pp. 13-14, Ex B,C	12	ES
F1-03	9/26	✓	15		Stack pp. 14-17, Ex A,B,C.	17	LB
F1-04	9/28		15		Stack pp. 18-24, Conver	18	ES

Fig. 9: Page of Tape Register Book

When tapes are planned, or when it is sure that a drill will be needed for a given lesson in the book, a number is assigned to the tape. The numbers are taken from the register, using as many numbers as needed. These numbers are reserved by entering them in the book in column 1 and initialing column 7; other information is filled in as the procedure advances.

The tape register book is kept in the recording studio, near the master tape recorder. When a number is needed for a new script, open the book to the correct language, course, and block, and take the next number(s). In Fig. 9 the next available number is F1-05.

All pages for a given language are together in the book. All the French pages are first, then all the German, then all the Russian, then Spanish, etc. Within each language the pages are arranged by numbers or blocks of numbers in serial order. Additional pages are inserted as needed.

When a master tape is erased, the number is crossed out of the register. The number is reported to the card cataloguer, who finds the script. The first page lists the main reference and cross-references for that tape.

5"	✓		Sept. 12, 1960		2
REEL SIZE	STUDENT	MASTER	DATE BEGUN	DATE ENDED	PAGE NO.

CODE: P=PURCHASED   E=ERASED   R=RECORDED

DATE	CODE	QUANTITY +	QUANTITY −	TOTAL	DATE	CODE	QUANTITY +	QUANTITY −	TOTAL
9/12/60	Balance forward			203		Balance forward			
9/13/60	E	14		217					
"	E	8		225					
9/18/60	P	30		255					
"	R		95	160					
"	R		18	142					
9/19/60	R		30	112					
"	E	22		134					

Fig. 10: Tape Inventory Page

The cards are found and removed, and the cataloguer checks the last square on the front page of the script (the "Withdrawn" line of the administrative checklist). The script is filed with other withdrawn scripts for future reference or possible re-recording at some later date.

C. Tape Inventory. A special page for inventory is kept for each type of tape and size of reel in stock. The inventory should show how many *blank* tapes remain available. When new tapes are bought, these are added to the running total; when tapes are used for copies or masters, the number used is subtracted from the running total. The final number on each page shows how many blank tapes can be used, and will indicate when blank stock must be replenished either by retiring tapes or by

Tape Number _____

TAPE NUMBER—FILING

COURSE _____ DATE _____
SUBJECT _____
    Cross–Reference _____
TEXT REFERENCE _____ pp. _____
Prepared by _____ Spoken by _____
Commercial recording reference _____

ADMINISTRATIVE CHECKLIST:
    Entered in register _____[Teacher]
    Card Catalogue: ( ) Subject   ( ) Cross-ref. [Cataloguer]
    Withdrawn from library on _____(date)

REMARKS:

"Tape _____ , _____ i
              [number]   [subject of drill]

reference _____
                    [book, page or section]

Instructions: (Anticipation drill) (repetition drill)

Join in as soon as you understand.

    1. M:[1]
       R:[2]
    2. M:
       R:
    3. M:
       R:

1 M = Master
2 R = Response

Fig. 11: Form for First Page of Tapescript

purchasing new ones. The assistants who make copies and erase tapes do most of the work on the inventory as a matter of routine; the director is the person who needs to know when the tape supply is dangerously low, so that he can request teachers to designate tapes for retirement or so that he can purchase more tapes.

D. Script Form—First Page. The first page of a script is always a form such as that shown in Fig. 11. The checklists and other pertinent information at the top assure the teacher and director that all the necessary functions have been completed. The lower half assures a uniform format in tape presentation. The tape number is shown at the top and (for ease of filing) along the edge. The second and third lines are for use of the cataloguer in preparing the cards. On the administrative checklist, the teacher checks the first square when the tape is entered in the register as "made," column 3. The cataloguer checks the second square when cards have been made and put in the catalogue. At this point the script would be filed. If the tape is withdrawn, the number is reported to the cataloguer who removes the appropriate cards from the catalogue, checks the third square, and files the script in the dead file.

E. Schedule for Library-Type Laboratory. In university laboratories where students arrange their own attendance hours, a schedule similar to that shown (Fig. 12) is posted for them to sign, or is used at a registration desk for assignment of hours. The schedule shows the time of beginning of each laboratory period, and has a number of blanks corresponding to the number of available booths.

F. Other Schedules. The director provides a simple sign-up sheet for teachers' use of the recording studio. Such a list could be posted near the studio, or on a central bulletin board.

In elementary and high school laboratories where classes attend the laboratory as a group, the usual method of assigning classrooms is used in assigning the laboratory to a class. The number of places remaining vacant each period should be noted. If the laboratory has 40 booths, but the class using it during a certain period has only 34 students, six booths can be made available (by sign-up) for students from study hall who want to work on their language assignment.

27. Supplies and Miscellaneous Equipment. The laboratory must have an adequate supply of tapes and such important equipment as splicers, rubber stamps, labels, and the like.

A. Tape Requirements. It is recommended that the 15-minute tape be a standard unit both for master and student tapes. For student tapes playing at the slow (3¾ i.p.s.) speed, this is one-half of a full 5-inch reel. For master tapes (at 7½ i.p.s.) it is a full 5-inch reel. Tape would therefore be purchased in 5-inch reels; Mylar and Tenzar tape are strongest.

LANGUAGE LABORATORY

Day of week	Day Month Year	
Supervisors 8:00 9:00 10:00 11:00	(12:00) 12:50 1:50 2:50	3:50 4:50

8:00 1 ... 9 ... 17
2 ... 10 ... 18
3 ... 11 ... 19
4 ... 12 ... 20
5 ... 13 ... 21
6 ... 14 ... 22
7 ... 15 ... 23
8 ... 16 ... 24

9:00 1 ... 9 ... 17
2 ... 10 ... 18
3 ... 11 ... 19
4 ... 12 ... 20
5 ... 13 ... 21
6 ... 14 ... 22
7 ... 15 ... 23
8 ... 16 ... 24

10:00 1 ... 9
2 ... 10
3
4
5

Fig. 12: Student Attendance Schedule
(for a 24-booth laboratory)

Student tapes are split; that is, for each full reel purchased, an empty 5-inch reel in a box is purchased. Half of the tape from the full reel is run onto the empty reel, and the tape is cut in the middle. This gives us two student reels. A length of white leader tape is spliced to the beginning of each of the two resulting half-full reels. The boxes and reels are stamped with the proprietary name of the laboratory, and the tapes are put in the blank stock supply. The quantity is added to the inventory sheet.

For an **initial supply of tape** only a rough estimate can be given. Enough to get started, with the understanding that more would be purchased as the inventory descends, might be about 10 full 5-inch reels (= 20 split reels) per booth. For example, with 40 booths, the estimate would be 400 full 5-inch reels (40 x 10). This estimate is for use of laboratories using the library system. If the laboratory has broadcasting facilities only, use the computation for master tapes. **Master tapes** may be secured for an initial supply on the basis of about five full 5-inch reels per booth. This is in addition to the supply of student tapes, if used. Master tapes are not split. For each master tape there should be a broadcasting (duplicate) master during the few days the tape is classified as a *current* lesson.

The rate of use of this initial tape supply should be studied so that further purchases can be based on actual experience in the laboratory.

B. Splicing Equipment. At least two good splicing machines * and a supply of splicing tape will be needed. The proper cutting angle, perfect matching of the tape edges, and a non-flowing adhesive are all automatic when such a splicing machine is used. Results are uniform, splices are tight, and time is conserved.

C. Leader Tape. Every tape in use should be prepared by splicing about 2½ feet of white plastic leader tape † on the leading end. This tape protects the magnetic tape, facilitates threading, and (in the case of masters) allows the tape number and other identification to be written directly on it with a ball-point pen.

D. Labels. All tapes are labeled with the number assigned. The number should be on the shelfback, usually on the edge of the box left blank by the manufacturer as a place to write the title. The labels should be placed in a uniform position. Rectangular self-adhesive labels in sheets ‡ are very satisfactory. The number is stamped on the correct number of labels while they are still on the waxed backing sheets. The labels are placed on the boxes during the time the tapes are being recorded.

* Robins TS4A-DLX Tape Splicer and half a dozen rolls of Robins ST-500 splicing tape would be a good choice.

† Scotch brand *Leader and Timing Tape* number 43P; or *Soundcraft* Mylar base colored leader tape, which comes in red, blue, yellow, and white, and is therefore very useful for identifying tapes used for different languages, master tapes, and special tapes. (Reeves Soundcraft Corp., 10 East 52nd Street, New York 22, N. Y.)

‡ Recommended: Avery adhesive label number S-602, rectangular (⅜ x 1¼ inches). This is available at office supply stores.

Rubber stamps having a letter on the first band, and several bands of numbers thereafter, can be purchased for this purpose.

E. Bulk Eraser. The bulk eraser is used to wipe all recorded sound off used tapes, restoring the tape to factory-fresh silence. Retired student tapes and broadcasting masters are quickly and efficiently erased for return to blank stock by use of this machine. The *Librascope Noiseraser* and the *Microtan HD-11 Bulk Tape Eraser* are two recommended instruments.

F. Head Demagnetizer. The recording heads of tape recorders gradually acquire some permanent magnetism. This causes tapes to sound noisy. The small and inexpensive instrument called a *head demagnetizer* is plugged into an electric outlet, the tip held for a moment at the gap of the recording head and then gradually withdrawn. This rids the recorder of the troublesome static until the magnetism builds up again. The heads should be cleaned with a special solvent and demagnetized periodically.

G. Marking Devices. A rubber stamp with the name of the laboratory, and special stamp-pad ink (*Justrite* "Slink" Opaque) are used to mark plastic reels and metallic objects.

China-marking pencils are useful for temporary identification of reels.

Colored self-adhesive dots (Avery Adhesive Label Co.) are used for coding master tapes in some laboratories. A green dot is affixed at the top of the shelfback on master tapes so that they can be quickly identified if one should stray into the student tape shelves. A red dot on a master tape indicates that there is sufficient unused tape on the reel for another recorded drill.

Classroom Procedures

THE CLASSROOM and the language laboratory are complementary parts of an efficient instructional system. The language laboratory is more economical of the student's time in the presentation of pattern and pronunciation drills requiring much repetition. The teacher is relieved of endless repetitions, while not being deprived of the ability to monitor individual students; and all students work actively during an entire laboratory period. Classroom time is now freed for preparing students to use the laboratory intelligently; and afterwards, for making use of the students' newly acquired fluency through flexibility drills and cultural studies in the foreign language. In short, the laboratory helps the student gather the building blocks of language; the classroom puts the building blocks to use by creating situations analogous to those of the foreign country and asking the student to build some meaningful structures. The classroom becomes a little extra-territorial segment of a country whose language is being studied, and the student is absorbed into the cultural and linguistic patterns of this simulated foreign land. The laboratory has equipped him to express himself correctly and without embarrassment in dealing with the other "natives"—and he can have quite a lot of fun in doing so.

The function of the classroom now has two laboratory-related phases: the **pre-laboratory** phase and the **post-laboratory** phase. Both phases usually exist in a single classroom period. The pre-laboratory work prepares the students to use the drills correctly by demonstrating the new grammatical point deductively, giving simple pointers that will help the student master the drills, and doing several pairs from the drills themselves. This will enable the teacher to see that everyone understands precisely what is expected in the laboratory. It will save time by eliminating the need for lengthy (and usually confusing) instruction on the tapes. The pre-laboratory phase need not take more than five or ten minutes at the end of a classroom period just preceding a laboratory period.

The post-laboratory phase is, in a sense, a test of the student's learning in the laboratory. It consists of confronting the student with the necessity of expressing himself by using the newly learned principle and all his previous experience in the language. This can be done by question-and-answer drills, situation drills, short lectures on cultural subjects containing frequent examples of the new point, dictation, and the like.

The class time is also used for the reading and writing objectives (except for students in grades lower than junior high school). Reading and writing lag behind aural-oral proficiency by a few days. Only when the teacher is sure that students have mastered a segment of work aurally and orally does he require them to learn the regular spelling of the things they have learned to *say*. Thus students might be working on the current lesson in a textbook *aurally* and *orally*, and be doing dictation and reading on the previous lesson.

A typical lesson plan for an elementary course might divide the class time among the following activities, in this order:

1. **Post-laboratory Exercises.** Flexibility drills based upon the most recent material prepared in the laboratory by the students.

2. **Reading and Writing Exercises.** Dictation based upon second-to-last laboratory work done by students. Students have mastered this material aurally and orally and have been assigned writing exercises.

    If possible, some non-graded dictation practice is first given in class (some students at the board, some using their own paper at their seats).

3. **Cultural Presentation.** A short cultural presentation in the form of a talk, filmstrip, song, or other segment of the total cultural pattern being taught. Students then participate. Use varied means of eliciting their oral co-operation and practice.

4. **Pre-laboratory Orientation.** The new grammatical or phonetic principle is presented, often deductively. If new sounds are involved the teacher gives exact instructions as to positions of the vocal organs and the production of sound.

    Brief samples of the drills to be expected in the next laboratory session are presented to the class. The teacher takes the part of the master track, and students respond first together and later individually.

The main consideration in classroom and laboratory methods, if the optimum sequence of presentation is to be followed, is that the students be *freed of reliance on written or printed symbols*. Visualization of printed words is to be avoided. The teacher resists attempts of students to find out how a new word is spelled until they have mastered the word completely on the phonetic level.

On the other hand, visualization of concrete *objects* is encouraged by the use of pictures and *realia* of all kinds. The purpose is to have the student make a direct association of the sound of the foreign word with

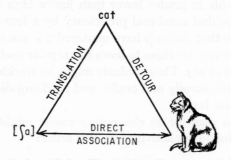

Fig. 13: Direct Aural-Visual Association

the object designated by it. When the French sound [lə ʃa] is uttered, the student should associate it directly with the animal, rather than the long way around indicated on the adjoining figure—first an association with an English word, *then* with the animal.

28. Introduction of Pronunciation. The first two recommended phases of any segment of instruction of foreign languages are *hearing* and *speaking*. The student first hears the sounds, then imitates the sounds. Hearing is not as simple as it appears to be because accurate and discriminating hearing is usually not a habit of most students. Speaking, or imitating the sounds heard, is also a complicated matter when some of the sounds are absolutely new to the student (because they do not exist in English). A few techniques for presenting pronunciation to beginning students in a foreign language are suggested here.

A point of departure is the identification of sounds that will be special teaching problems. These are sounds not normally used in English, such as [r] in French (*uvular* [r]) and in Spanish (*trilled*). Sounds calling for close rounding and protrusion of the lips (such as [ɔ] in French) are not common in English and need special teaching. Some fricatives (such as that in *Ich* in German) are difficult for English speakers.

Students will have no difficulty hearing and saying sounds that are already part of their native language. This is to be taken advantage of by the teacher; at the same time the teacher should make a list of difficult sounds and devise a method of instructing the students to produce them.

A. Hearing. It is not enough to say to a Spanish class, "Listen: *la vaca.* Repeat: *la vaca,*" or in a French class to say, "Listen: *la rue.* Repeat: *la rue.*" These words contain sounds that differ from the corresponding and apparently similar English sounds. The student must be made keenly aware of the differences before he attempts a pronunciation. The contrasting-pair method is one that can be used.

The teacher says the foreign word-group twice, one time correctly, and one time inserting the equivalent English sound. The students play "same-or-different" by saying "same" or "different" as the game progresses:

TEACHER: (*showing a picture representing the idea* street): Listen to the French word for "street": *la rue. la rue. la rue.* [ry]

To see if you can recognize this sound [y] in the word [ry], let's play "same-or-different." I'll say a pair of words. If they are the same, say "same." If they're different, say "different."

Listen: [la ry]—[la ru].

STUDENTS: Different!

TEACHER: They were different. Next pair: [la ru]—[la ru].
STUDENTS: Same!

TEACHER: Same. [la ru]—[la ry] . . . etc.

When the students have thus been started on their training as critical listeners, the teacher asks them to identify the correct word for *street:*

TEACHER: (*showing picture for street*): Now I'll say two words, one of which is correct for "street" in French. If the first word is correct, say "first"; if the second is correct, say "second." Listen: [la ru]—[la ry].
STUDENTS: Second!

TEACHER: Second is right. Again: [la ru]—[la ru].
STUDENTS: Neither!

TEACHER: Good! Neither was right. Again: [la ry]—[la ru].
STUDENTS: First!

TEACHER: First is right. Now that you can hear the French sounds for this word accurately, it is time to learn how to *say* the word. . . .

[NOTE: *This colloquy is continued in the section on teaching pronunciation to follow.*]

The technique was first to *contrast* sounds by inserting an English sound in the foreign word. When a distinction could be made by the students, the teacher became more specific, asking for the *identification* of the proper sound.

Another method used after the students have learned the pronunciation of some words is to give a pair of words. One member of the pair contains an error. The students repeat the correct word:

TEACHER: Now let's see if you know the gender of some nouns, and know the difference between *le* and *la:* **le classe, la classe.**
STUDENTS: la classe.

TEACHER: la classe.   [CORRECT ANSWER]
STUDENTS: la classe.   [REPETITION]

TEACHER: **le chat, la chat.**
STUDENTS: le chat.

TEACHER: le chat.
STUDENTS: le chat. etc. . . .

When students have learned to answer a simple question like "What's this?" or "This is a cat, isn't it?" the following exercise is effective in sharpening critical hearing, drilling on genders, and perfecting pronunciation and intonation. The teacher shows a visual stimulus (a picture or real object within the vocabulary experience of the students). Making an error in pronunciation, or pronouncing correctly, he asks the class if he is identifying the object shown. If he errs, the students correct him. The correct and incorrect statements of the teacher are mixed in random fashion. Anticipation form is used to assure that students repeat the correct answers:

TEACHER: (*showing picture of street*): C'est **le** rue, n'est-ce pas?
STUDENTS: Non, monsieur (mademoiselle, madame), c'est **la** rue.

TEACHER: C'est la rue.
STUDENTS: C'est la rue.

TEACHER (*showing picture of cat*): C'est le chat, n'est-ce pas?
STUDENTS: Oui, monsieur (mademoiselle, madame), c'est le chat.

TEACHER: C'est le chat.
STUDENTS: C'est le chat. . . . etc.

It will be seen that adequate training in hearing requires more than simply saying the new word once or twice, and then launching into pronunciation. The habit of careful auditory discrimination can be developed through exercises such as this. In the last exercise above, variations can be introduced by making pronunciation errors other than those of gender. For instance, in the first exchange the teacher could show the picture of the street and say, "C'est la roue [ru], n'est-ce pas?" (*It's the wheel, isn't it?*), using the close but incorrect sound in the word for *street*. Students who had learned to listen carefully would make the correction, "Non, monsieur, c'est la rue."

Such hearing drills are kept short and are usually limited to the new sounds about to be presented for pronunciation.

B. Speaking. As soon as the students have learned to identify the new sound positively, and to discern it from other sounds that are close and likely to be confused with it, the hearing phase is momentarily replaced by the speaking phase of instruction. People cannot necessarily reproduce a sound merely because they can recognize it. Students must be given rather specific physiological information. They must be told exactly where the tip and blade of the tongue should be in relation to the teeth and palate; what lip position is to be assumed, as, for example, whether to grin widely (*spread*), pout like a goldfish (*close rounded, protruded*); whether the jaw is wide open, nearly closed, or at half-mast. In other words, each student is assisted in putting his resonating chamber (*vocal organs*) in the correct arrangement for making the desired sound. Good will and a sound to imitate are not enough alone.

(1) Mouth Position Drills. Often students have no clear idea of the position of the tongue or of the shape of the mouth in making sounds. The physiological instructions will not be very effective if the student cannot carry them out. Make students aware of the position of the tongue by such drills as this: to demonstrate the importance of the tongue position and its intense influence on the quality of sound, have students sound an [l] with the tip of the tongue at the upper front teeth—in a word like *balcony*. Then they try the same word, this time producing [l] with the tip of the tongue as far back on the roof of the mouth as possible. The clarity of the first sound contrasts sharply with the muddiness of the last. Have the students try [l] starting with the tongue at the correct (for French) position, tip at the upper incisors, and while continuing to voice the sound, gradually run the tongue back along the roof of the mouth. This will make them aware of the tongue position, give practice in control, and emphasize the importance of precise positioning for sound production. Other similar exercises may be devised for this purpose.

(2) **First Pronunciation Drills.** Sounds are first introduced for *speaking* as part of a word or word-group. Yet accurate production of each individual sound is important at this stage. One way to solve this problem is related to the noun-unit pronunciation drills (§ 29A). A word containing the sound to be taught is selected. This word is represented by a simple drawing on a card. The picture is shown, the word is presented for hearing as described above, and then taught syllable by syllable to the class.

As an example, suppose the word l'église is to be taught. A card showing a church is displayed, and the word l'église is repeated by the teacher several times. Then the syllables are taken up one at a time. There are, in this case, two syllables and an extra consonant sound:

$$[le \quad gli \quad z]$$
$$1 \qquad 2$$

Rather than asking the students to say [le], then [gli], then [z], then the whole word, a different technique is suggested: teach the syllables sound by sound, **beginning at the wrong end** of each syllable:

SYLLABLE	*but* TEACHER SAYS:	STUDENTS:
[le] (*first*)	[e]	[e]
	[le]	[le]
[gli] (*second*)	[i]	[i]
	[li]	[li]
	[gli]	[gli]
	[z]	[z]
[le gli z]	[le gli z]	[le gli z]

The device of approaching difficult combinations of consonants by beginning at the vowel and adding the consonants one at a time *in front* of it is helpful in most languages. Even though (as in English) a syllable may not end in a vowel, the backwards development of such combinations is of assistance.

(3) **Sound Production Methods.** Exact physiological instructions are given so that students have their vocal organs in correct position for sound imitation.

New sounds can be built from old familiar ones. Progression from the known to the unknown is an old teaching adage. For instance, English speakers do not know how to produce the French **u** [y], the German **ü** [y]. However, they have no difficulty in learning to grin broadly and utter an excellent [i], so the teacher directs a drill to have the students sound [i] while a new position of the mouth is taken up. If the familiar sound [i] is uttered while the mouth is closely rounded and protruded (the goldfish—*or even* swordfish look) the resultant sound is the desired [y]. Here is the method which may be adapted to other similar problems:

> TEACHER: Now we have learned that [y] can be identified in the same-or-different drill. Let's try to produce the sound ourselves. Say [i] with a big, happy grin: [i].
>
> STUDENTS: [i]
>
> TEACHER: A bigger grin this time. Repeat: [i]—[i].
>
> STUDENTS (*grinning*): [i]—[i].
>
> TEACHER: Now we will say [i]—[i] again in exactly that rhythm, but change from a grin to goldfish for the second [i]. Round your lips as if you were whistling and protrude them far forward. I'll snap my fingers after the first [i] to remind you goldfish to appear. Ready. [i].
>
> STUDENTS: [i]
>
> TEACHER (*snaps fingers*).
>
> STUDENTS (*much surprised by the sound that emanates from the goldfish*): [y].
>
> TEACHER: Again: [i] (*snaps fingers*) [y]. . . . etc.

Application of the new sound is made immediately in words containing it and other sounds already known: *la lune, la fusée,* etc., using pictures for visual association at the same time.

A blackboard drawing is helpful in reminding the students of the change in mouth position that must be made. In the sequence [i]—[i] a sketch such as this might be placed on the board:

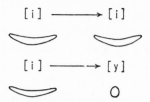

Fig. 14: Mouth Position Reminder

The repetition of the symbol [i] reminds them that they are attempting to make the same sound in each case; the crescent and the circle represent the grin and the goldfish mouth positions. The teacher points to them in turn as the sounds are uttered.

Ingenuity needs to be exercised to find ways of using known sounds to create the new ones required in the foreign language. The teacher will come upon such devices as the one just described. The student must make a conscious effort to assume the correct position of vocal organs when he makes these sounds, just as a person learning the touch system of typing must for a time think about what finger goes where. Later the fingers automatically go to the right places. Similarly, in speaking the foreign language the vocal organs will eventually assume the correct positions for making certain sounds automatically. Until the student reaches that point he must not be allowed to relax his efforts. To do so is to slip back into the ingrained habits of the native language. The student *can* learn to speak the foreign language without traces of an English accent if he makes a persistent effort in this regard. He must also attend to the differences in rhythm, stress, and intonation. These nuances of pronunciation are easily gained from laboratory drills.

The importance of pre-laboratory orientation is clear, especially at the outset of the study of a foreign language. The physiological descriptions are best given in person so that the teacher can observe and correct errors at once. After the students have an idea of how to go about producing the sounds, they can profit by the laboratory repetition drills.

29. The Material of Basic Pronunciation Drills. There are two effective methods of introducing pronunciation and of giving systematic drill of a repetitive yet interesting nature. These methods we may call the *noun-unit* method and the *sentence-unit* method. The objective of both is to give students adequate practice in pronunciation (rhythm, stress, and intonation included) in sense-making patterns. Both rely heavily upon question-and-answer drills.

A. Noun-Unit Method. Select about 30 nouns from the first few lessons of the textbook. These nouns should be equally divided among the various types (masculine, feminine, those beginning with a vowel if this makes a difference, etc.); they should represent concrete objects or people; they should collectively contain all the sounds of the language being taught. To facilitate presentation, they should be easily represented by a simple line drawing on a 9 x 11 card.

Let us suppose that the array of cards in Fig. 15 represents the group selected for pronunciation drill for a given textbook. Notice that a few verbs have been represented as abstractions in the verb column, and that these abstractions are meaningful by agreement with the students. Each card represents *only one thing.* For example, the card for *cage* is never used for *bird,* although there is a bird in the cage.

Individual cards are selected for the most elementary introduction of sounds through hearing and guided pronunciation work as described in the preceding section. Cards representing words having easy sounds are used first, then more difficult ones. Other cards using the same sounds are grouped with the card used for introducing the sound. The student learns the word in association with the visual stimulus. The questions "What is this?" and "This is a—, isn't it?" are used by the teacher, and the student is taught the foreign language of "It's the—" for reply. Thus the vocabulary is learned in an elementary conversational exchange based on visual stimuli. After all the nouns have been taught for initial teaching of individual sounds, they are arranged in *patterned* order (all masculine nouns together, all feminine, all those beginning with vowels). Figure 15 has the nouns arranged in patterned order for French.

Four cards are set on the blackboard ledge for the next phase of instruction, which we might call *ringing the changes.* We are ready to represent ideas visually, and have the student state the ideas in the foreign language. Line one of Fig. 15 might be the first arrangement. Cards are set up in the word-order required. Initial drill would be to make the statement corresponding to the series of pictures. At change 1 students repeat: **Le chat / arrive / à la maison / à midi** (*The cat arrives at the house*

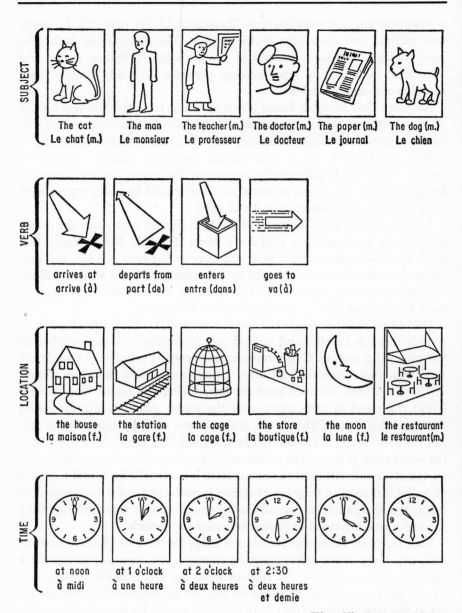

Fig. 15: Pronunciation

The lady	The letter	The flower	The car	The policeman	The bird
La dame (f.)	La lettre (f.)	La fleur (f.)	L'auto (f.)	L'agent (m.)	L'oiseau (m.)

the garden	the castle	the school	the hotel	the church
le jardin (m.)	le château (m.)	l'école (f.)	l'hôtel (m.)	l'église (f.)

Drill Cards

at noon.). Questions corresponding to the following are then asked (in the foreign language) in the order indicated:

1. **Does** the cat arrive at the house at noon?
2. The cat arrives at the house at noon, **doesn't he?**
3. **Who** arrives at the house at noon?
4. **Where** does the cat arrive at noon?
5. **At what time** does the cat arrive at the house?

The purpose of this is to present first the questions that contain the full answer (*est-ce que* and *n'est-ce pas* types in French, *verdad* in Spanish, *nicht wahr* in German, etc.). Questions 3 through 5 omit an element of the statement that the student must supply. Intonation, word-grouping into sense-making groups, and numbers are learned in this way.

As soon as the original sequence has been done by the class as a whole, a change is made. The second card (the man) is dropped in place over the original subject (the cat), and a new sentence develops. The same kinds of questions are asked. Subject cards are rotated systematically through the subject column. Then the contractions are taught by rotating the cards in the LOCATION column. In French, German, and Spanish the preposition and article form a contraction at certain times. Patterning of the nouns (in French, first feminine nouns requiring no contractions, then masculine nouns requiring them) allows deductive teaching when the first contraction is reached. In Fig. 15 the contractions are taught with *à* using *arrive;* when the time comes to change to the verb *part,* contractions with *de* will be taught.

Because each column is systematically changed a great number of combinations is possible, and the *situation* is constantly changing. As in real life, one never knows what to expect. If we happen upon "The cat arrives at the moon at noon," nothing is lost grammatically; it makes sense, allows practice in oral composition (the students will be able by then to look at the visual situation and make a statement about it without need for the teacher to coach them), and such unexpected situations are amusing—they keep the class lively and entertaining.

When the material and structure taught thus have been mastered orally, the students are ready to learn how to write the sentences they can say. Reading follows as a natural consequence. Dictation is used.

Oral composition is started by use of such cards. Students can tell simple stories based on several sequences of such cards. Then a single card with several figures (perhaps a picture of a man arriving at the station, taken from a magazine advertisement) can be talked about. One card is shown the class. Each student contributes a statement about the picture. Then the statements are organized orally and later written.

Adjectives are added to the student's repertory, and the people and animals in the cards are given names. We then develop the basic sentence in Fig. 15 to

> The *young* man arrives at the *big white* house at noon.
> The man's *name is* Albert Dupont, and he is a policeman.
> He goes to the cage. The *little* cat is looking at the cage. etc.

The noun-unit method provides a good command of the building blocks of language, is extremely flexible and capable of sustaining interest, simulates real life through visual presentation of continually changing situations, and leads naturally into oral composition, conversation, and reading and writing skills. New cards are always being added to the collection by the teacher, and more complicated arrangements (e.g. a series of *two* simple card-statements to be composed into a complex sentence using a relative pronoun) can be organized for advanced grammar. Verb tenses can be changed ("The man *entered* the house at noon" or "The man *will enter* the house at noon tomorrow" etc.).

At present the teacher has to make his own cards. It is hoped that soon publishers will have a usable set to accompany texts. Filmstrips are another possibility in projecting all four cards at once; the second frame would ring one change, and so on. A final suggestion for laboratory use: pages such as Fig. 15 could be duplicated without any captions and used in conjunction with tape drills, using substitution:

> 1. Repeat: The man arrives at the house at noon. #
>   STUDENT: The man arrives at the house at noon. #
>
> 2. The cat . . . #
>   STUDENT: The cat arrives at the house at noon. #
>
> 3. The doctor . . . #
>   STUDENT: The doctor arrives at the house at noon. #
>
> 12. . . . at the station #
>   STUDENT: The doctor arrives at the station at noon. #

Or again, dwelling on one arrangement of pictures for a few moments, the tape could pose the same questions originally asked in class ("*Who* arrives at the station at noon?"). The student responds, basing his answers on the latest change; the anticipation drill is used so that the student always has an opportunity to check and repeat correct responses.

B. Sentence-Unit Method. A second method for teaching pronunciation is to devise a number of fixed statements. These statements must contain all the sounds of the language, and should all relate to one subject. One such arrangement consists of three graded sentences; the first contains easy sounds, the second and third more difficult ones.

If, for example, the first sentence-unit were *Madame Doucet habite Calais,* the words would be introduced one by one, sound by sound. Then questions of the same type as before are used:

1. **Does** Madame Doucet live in Calais?
2. Madame Doucet lives in Calais, **doesn't she?**
3. **Who** lives in Calais?
4. **Where** does Madame Doucet live?

Then a second sentence is presented, and further questions based on it. This continues until enough sentences have been learned to teach all the sounds. At the end of oral mastery of each sentence, students are given the regular spelling and required to learn to write it.

The same purposes are served by this method as by the other, except that this method lacks the flexibility and desirable patterning of the noun-unit method. While students are expected to be able to substitute other nouns in the place of "Madame Doucet" and "Calais," they usually do not get systematic practice in so doing under this method. The building blocks they need for expressing their own thoughts are never sufficiently organized or established.

30. Visual Coupled Drills. Using visual stimuli for speaking the foreign language is far superior to presenting an idea in English (spoken or written) for "translation." Once the pronunciation, rhythm, accent, and intonation have been taught by the noun-unit or sentence-unit method, the teacher turns to devices for organizing speech into larger patterns of thought. The visual coupled drill is a systematic way of eliciting a series of sentences, all joined together in a larger "story."

A description of the day's activities of a student is a convenient and useful form for narrative. Students are provided with a duplicated page showing the activities in order of their occurrence (Fig. 16, *Albert's Day*). This page is useful throughout the elementary course, and is adaptable to teaching new verb tenses, times, and other useful relationships.

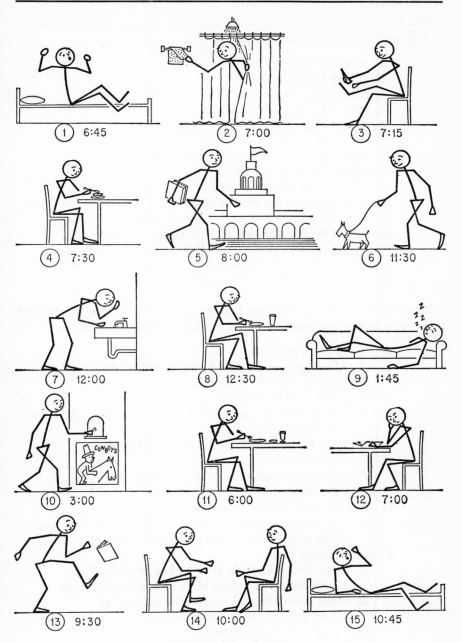

Fig. 16: Albert's Day

The full sequence of events as portrayed in this particular version is as follows, using the present tense:

1. Albert gets up at 6:45.
2. Albert bathes at 7:00.
3. Albert gets dressed at 7:15.
4. Albert has breakfast at 7:30.
5. Albert arrives at school at 8:00.
6. Albert goes for a walk at 11:30.
7. Albert washes his hands and face at noon.
8. Albert has lunch at 12:30.
9. Albert rests a little at 1:45.
10. Albert goes to the movies at 3:00.
11. Albert has supper at 6:00 in the evening.
12. Albert begins studying at 7:00 in the evening.
13. Albert finishes studying at 9:30 in the evening.
14. Albert chats with his friends at 10:00 in the evening.
15. Albert goes to bed at 10:45 in the evening.

This drill is made available on tape in the laboratory for the student to learn. Some of the patterns based on this drill are given below:

A. First-Person Pattern:
    1. Albert **gets up** at 6:45 in the morning. And you? #
    I **get up** at 6:45 in the morning too. #
B. Third-Person Plural Pattern:
    2. Albert **bathes** at 7:00 in the morning. And your friends? #
    They **bathe** at 7:00 in the morning too. #
C. Past Tense Drill:
    3. Albert **got dressed** at 7:15 yesterday. And you? #
    I **got dressed** at 7:15 yesterday too. #
D. Future Tense Drill:
    4. Albert **will have** breakfast tomorrow at 7:30. And you? #
    I'll have breakfast tomorrow at 7:30 too. #
E. Relationship Drills:
    5. What does Albert do after he has breakfast? #
    Albert arrives at school **after** he has breakfast. #
    2. What does Albert do before he bathes? #
    Albert gets up **before** he bathes. #
F. Time and Activity Questions:
    4. What does Albert do at 7:30 in the morning? #
    Albert has breakfast at 7:30 in the morning. #

9. When does Albert rest a little? #
Albert rests a little at 1:45 in the afternoon. #
4. What do you do at 7:30 in the morning? #
I have breakfast at 7:30 in the morning. #
10. When do you go to the movies? #
I go to the movies at 3:00 in the afternoon. #
12. At what time did you begin studying last night? #
I began studying at 7:00 last night. #
9. What were you doing when your father came in at 1:45 in the afternoon? #
I was resting a bit when **he came in** at 1:45. #

This sheet will serve to teach verbs in all persons and tenses. Negation can be introduced, requiring two statements in response:

G. Negation:
1. Did Albert get up at 7:00 yesterday morning? #
No, he didn't get up at 7:00; he got up at 6:45 yesterday morning. #

Although only one or two examples of each pattern are shown, the pattern may be carried straight through the entire sequence of 15 pictures. All drills can be taught in the laboratory. Post-laboratory drills in class may include oral composition—the student tells the entire sequence for Albert, for his parents, for himself, for you. Then the student may later tell about his own day as it actually exists. This oral composition may be embroidered with further details learned in the meantime: what the weather was like when he got up; when it started raining; when the sun set; whom he met during the day; where they went, and so on. When each segment of the work is mastered orally, dictation is used to teach writing and reading.

Similar coupled drills may take other forms such as filmstrip presentation. The principle of the drills remains much the same whether used in conjunction with a printed sheet or with a projected picture. Filmstrips are excellent in the laboratory, projected high enough to be seen above the booth tops (the "drop fronts" do not overcome the blinder effect, narrow range of side vision, and heads of students in booths ahead as obstacles to view). There the equipment can be installed permanently.

31. Other Methods and Aids. Some other classroom techniques that enable students to express themselves, thus putting the foreign language to use, are: situation drills, songs, games, plays, oral reports. Aural prac-

tice is further acquired by use of recordings, films, and filmstrips with correlated sound tracks.

A. Situation Drills. Simulated real-life situations are set up in the classroom, often using "props." Conversation manuals and many textbooks propose situations that can be used or adapted. Situations should be kept simple at first, and short enough that certain patterns of speech are well learned. An example of a situation is as follows:

> Albert has just arrived in Berlin, and meets a classmate. Albert invites his friend to have coffee in a nearby *café*.

This drill requires two actors with a knowledge of greetings, small talk about "back home," and simple useful inquiries. Students will enjoy preparing and presenting their versions. Vocabulary that may be needed for a situation drill is presented by the teacher in noun-unit type pronunciation drills before the situation is assigned.

B. Songs, Games, Plays. Especially useful for elementary school children, and hardly diminishing at higher levels in interest content, are songs and games. Folksongs and popular current songs give a feeling for the distinctive culture being studied. They furnish a framework for pronunciation practice; but it should be remembered that the pronunciation of a language as applied to music may differ considerably from conversational pronunciation.

Games, from simple children's games to more sophisticated ones such as spelling bees, Twenty Questions, and the like, furnish an opportunity for spontaneous self-expression in the foreign language. Numbers may be taught by variations of Bingo (*Tengo* in Spanish, *Je l'ai* in French), particularly successful in FLES programs. In high schools and colleges having more advanced classes, parliamentary procedure in clubs is a form of game.

Theatrical productions and skits in the foreign language are ambitious undertakings, requiring many hours of outside preparation and involving a rather small number of students. It is an activity not ordinarily within the scope of classroom teaching. In some large universities a foreign-language play is a regular annual feature; it is an entirely voluntary activity for both staff and students.

C. Oral Reports. Oral reports are free composition in the spoken language, and are possible even on the elementary level. Students might be asked to describe and explain the use of some simple object (a pencil, a book, a clock, a radio), using a sketch or the object itself. Reports of a cultural nature include descriptions and explanations of famous land-marks and buildings of the country being studied, and studies of customs, festivals, industries, music, politics, science, and art. Students will do some research on the subject of their choice, express the ideas simply, answer class questions after their presentation, and thus contribute to the cultural program of the course.

D. Films. Specially prepared films for teaching modern languages have been placed on the market. Carefully controlled vocabulary and gram-matical structuring have been combined with excellent acting talent, authentic cultural atmosphere, and photographic merit. However, these films are not one-hour affairs if used for teaching purposes. Careful preparation is essential. The makers of the films often furnish copies of the shooting scripts and advice to the teacher. Several hours of class preparation for vocabulary and grammatical and idiomatic points are required if full benefit is to be derived. This preparation should be of the aural-oral kind (*not* by use of a written script).

Other films may be selected on a purely one-time basis for transmitting cultural and factual information about the foreign country. The Embassy of the country might be contacted to secure the free sound films they have for just this purpose.

Some schools have projectors with magnetic sound track devices. Students secure a cultural film, to which a magnetic blank track is com-mercially applied. The project for the students is to write their own foreign language commentary, apply their narration to the film, and present the completed product for the class to see. This is a drill for advanced students.

E. Filmstrips. Special filmstrips for first-year presentation and for second-year review are available using the anticipation mode and struc-tured pattern drills. These filmstrips last about 12 minutes, and can be used with synchronized tapes and projectors. As a picture of a restaurant opposite a garage appears on the screen, the tape is heard:

1. Where is the restaurant? #
 The restaurant is **opposite** the garage. #

The next frame of the filmstrip automatically advances to a picture of the same street, but now the garage is blank, and there is a hotel next to the restaurant:

2. Where is the hotel? #
 The hotel is **next to** the restaurant. #

This type of drill (here, dealing with prepositions and positions) continues for about 30 frames. Then there is a complete review followed by a testing phase.

The teacher can prepare similar drills with other commercially made filmstrips, both culturally and grammatically oriented.

There are some drawbacks to films and filmstrips. Unless the classroom is permanently equipped with the necessary projectors and associated equipment, the teacher must carry a screen, projector, recorder, synchronizer, extension cord, and audio cables from one room to another. The room must be darkened, the equipment set up and operated, and then taken down and moved again. This formidable task discourages many teachers from the use of filmstrips and movies. The best solution (administrators take note!) is to have every classroom equipped permanently with all the necessary apparatus, including efficient blinds for darkening the room totally and remote controls for the teacher's use.

These are some of the methods for introducing pronunciation and developing in the student the ability to express himself accurately, immediately, and with native fluency and pronunciation. Methods for the next two objectives—reading and writing—are discussed in the next chapter.

VIII

Reading and Writing Objectives

READING and writing are introduced progressively as instruction proceeds, lagging a lesson or two behind the current material being taught aurally and orally. No reading or writing is ever presented until the teacher is convinced that students have thoroughly mastered the material phonetically: that they can understand instantaneously what is said in the foreign language up to that point of instruction, and can accurately produce meaningful utterances. Then the secondary skill of reading is taught by various techniques to be described here, and the more difficult ability to write the foreign language is developed.

Programs in the elementary schools frequently defer the teaching of reading and writing. Children who begin a foreign language in the grades, and who continue the language (as they should) into high school will quickly master those skills when they are introduced at that level. By that time they will have had considerable practice in self-expression and "free composition," and their need for formal analytical grammar will be small—they will be able to compose the natural and correct flow of language in writing by reference to what they normally say, rather than by reference to "rules." This is a desirable aim at *all* levels of instruction. Pattern drills for oral use are designed to achieve such a result.

32. Reading. Reading is of two major kinds: the reading aloud of written material and the silent reading for content only. Reading aloud is useful—radio announcers, actors, public speakers, and the like must all reconvert written symbols into their oral prototype. The result must sound natural. *Silent reading* requires the use of eyes independently of the tongue; in fact, efficient silent reading is greatly hindered if the reader *verbalizes* (silently pronounces everything he reads, forming his vocal organs correctly for speech and sometimes actually making the sounds). The teacher must set the objective for the moment and concentrate on it. Rapid silent reading is a skill needed by persons doing *extensive* reading, and is therefore especially needed by advanced students, e.g. in literary studies.

Reading aloud seems the logical starting point for beginning and intermediate courses. In this process the student learns the sometimes tricky relationships between what he knows how to say, and the written symbols that represent those ideas. He is just becoming accustomed to the structure of the language and to its vocabulary. He needs to move cautiously in the forest of symbols until the paths become familiar. Later on, he can run through them rapidly, for he will have learned to take in at a glance things that are now strange and complicated.

Generally, reading should not mean translation into English. Translation may be used as an exercise for advanced students, but is a real impediment to the use of the foreign language as a self-sufficient means of communication at the beginner's level.

The main difficulties for an English-speaking student in making the transition to reading *seem* to be those relating to symbols *not* used in English. The student of Russian must learn the Cyrillic alphabet (not a difficult task in fact), the student of Arabic must learn a tremendously complex system of writing, and German students may be required to learn to read Fraktur. When the alphabet used is Roman, the problem is diminished somewhat. However, there may be new signs and symbols added to those letters with which the student is familiar: accented letters (ü, é, ñ, etc.), special combinations (ß, in German, for example), ligatures (œ). Yet these are minor problems. The biggest problem, if the alphabet is Roman, is preventing the student from assigning English values to familiar letters. His past and relatively long experience in reading English causes him automatically to lapse into English sounds that he equates with these familiar symbols. Upon seeing the French *finir,* students tend to give the letter *i* the sound of *i* in *it;* yet this sound does not exist in French. What is true for *i* is also true for a great many other familiar letters.

This is one of the principal reasons for insisting on aural-oral mastery before the printed or written representation of a word or phrase is shown. Once the student has a firm grip on the sound of a word, he is less likely to be influenced to mispronounce it on the basis of the symbols. Thus if the Spanish student knows how to say *llegar,* he will not be likely to pronounce it with [1] when he eventually sees it in writing in a familiar context. Similarly, the student of French will not suddenly begin to pronounce the final *t* of *le chat* (cat) when he learns that is the way it is written.

Another important reason for deferring presentation of writing until after phonetic mastery is the tendency of our students to be visually oriented with regard to words. The first question usually occurring when they hear a new word is "How do you spell that?" They feel that there may be a sound they are missing, and that the spelling will reveal it. Yet we have seen what a pitfall the spelling can be. A solution to this is the oral presentation, syllable by syllable, and particularly using the reversal method explained in § 28B (2) for syllables having difficult sound combinations. This approach assures the student that he is hearing each and every *sound* (since only one sound at a time, cumulatively, is added). At the same time it gradually frees him from the ponderous mental process of converting sounds to mental images of letters, then into articulation. When the student imitates a sound, it should be directly rather than through a visualization of written forms.

A. Classroom Preparation. Classroom preparation for reading may be considered pre-laboratory orientation because a great deal of reading training is most efficiently done in the laboratory.

Oral mastery of a sentence having been gained through basic pronunciation drills (like the noun-unit method, § 29A), the student is given his first glimpse of the way in which the words are normally printed. This can be in conjunction with the pronunciation drill cards already used. The word may be printed on the back of each picture. The student is shown a picture of *the house*. The teacher asks what it is. The student responds with the correct sounds, by now very familiar to him. The card is turned over, and the student repeats the word, observing the spelling. This is a flash card technique.

Next, one of the familiar arrangements of the pronunciation drill cards is used. A familiar array ("The man / arrives / at the house / at noon") is shown in pictures, and the backs of the cards are turned one at a time until the sentence stands in writing.

Rapid substitution of a printed word in an otherwise pictorial array is another variation. For example, a four-unit sentence is displayed, using three pictures and one printed word. If the printed word is the subject of the sentence, other printed words can be substituted in quick succession, and the students make each new statement aloud. They are now forced to rely on the printed word to complete the statement. New SUBJECT cards bearing words are dropped into place in rapid succession, and the class reads the printed word and completes the sentence-idea, using pictures as in basic pronunciation drill. Rapid recognition is possible. Accuracy of their reading is verified by the teacher, who turns the word card over to show the picture; the teacher then repeats the sentence.

Other elements of the pictorial array of cards are replaced by words, and gradually whole ideas are indicated in words.

The teacher may well point out the relationship of the printed word to the sound. Indicate deductively what letters are silent (as the students look at *le chat,* for instance, ask how the final *t* is pronounced; the combination *ch;* the *a*). As other words are introduced, bring up consistencies of spelling vis-à-vis sound. In Spanish, for instance, we have seen *llegar* with the *ll* pronounced [j]; when *llamarse* appears, the consistency of the pronunciation of the double-l becomes clearer. When dictation is shortly introduced, this information will be of value.

B. Laboratory Drills for Reading. Training in the reading phase can be continued in the laboratory. Tapes are prepared for material already done aurally and orally. Students are furnished printed texts of the material to be read—either as available in the textbook or specially prepared duplicated sheets.

(1) Built-up Drills. The student has the text before him in the booth. The tape used is a two-phase repetition drill. In the teaching phase the student hears the first sense-making group (such as *The young man*), and he repeats this precisely in a pause provided. The tape gives the next sense-making group (*arrives at the big white house*), and again a pause is allowed for the student's repetition. The final group in this sentence is given (*at three o'clock in the afternoon*), and the student repeats. This process continues throughout the reading exercise.

The testing phase of this drill reverts to the anticipation mode, as follows:

> *You will hear the number of the sentence to be read. As soon as the number is announced, read the sentence aloud onto the tape. You will then hear the sentence correctly read, and you will then repeat the sentence.*

1. MASTER: **Numéro 1.**
   STUDENT (*reads*): Le jeune homme arrive.

   MASTER: **Le jeune homme arrive.**
   STUDENT: Le jeune homme arrive.

2. MASTER: **Numéro 2.**
   STUDENT: Le jeune homme arrive à la maison.

   MASTER: **Le jeune homme arrive à la maison.**
   STUDENT: Le jeune homme arrive à la maison.

3. MASTER: **Numéro 3.**
   STUDENT: Le jeune homme arrive à la grande maison blanche.

   MASTER: **Le jeune homme arrive à la grande maison blanche.**
   STUDENT: Le jeune homme arrive à la grande maison blanche.

This procedure involves building up to the full sentence, adding a sense-making group at a time.

Sentences must be kept relatively short. Nothing is gained by lengthening sentences to unwieldy proportions. Stress is laid upon the division of sentences into *sense-making units,* upon exact duplication of the *intonation* of the master track, and upon imitation of the exact *speed and rhythm* of the master track.

(2) **Coaching Drills.** When the student has advanced beyond the elementary systematically built-up drills, he moves on to reading connected passages in the reading exercises—either in his text or in a reader. The laboratory coaching tape takes the place of time-wasting classroom monitoring of reading. The teacher prepares the tape by examining the reading assignment, making a slash-mark in the book after every relatively short sense-making group, and reading the assignment onto the tape. Pauses are left sufficient for repetition. Reading long complete sentences on the tape is not practical, as the student must be able to remember easily the sounds just heard. Sense-making groups are always the basis for these coaching drills, unless the complete sentence is very short.

Laboratory procedure for use of coaching drills would follow this sequence: (1) student uses the tape with book closed as a repetition drill, listening carefully for comprehension, and repeating with attention to accent, intonation, and sound production; (2) student opens book and uses tape for repetition drill; (3) student repeats the tape, this time reading each sense-making group *before* the group is read on the tape, as an anticipation drill. The latter tactic is merely a shift in the use of the pause in the tape. In repetition drill, the student reads during the pause *following* the master; in anticipation drill he uses the pause *before* the master to read from the book, then hears the master read the same sense-making group as a check.

C. Word Grouping. Transition to printed matter was made soon after each pronunciation unit. (It is advisable to prepare for reading by making sure that there are no words or expressions in the reading text that have not first been presented orally.) Built-up drills are used first, then coaching drills. Both are based on the *sense-making group,* or breath-group. Pre-laboratory orientation in class assures the teacher that students know how to use these tapes.

Just as basic pronunciation drills stressed the sense-making group forced on them by the visual stimuli, reading practice must elicit sense-making groups if the characteristics of normal speech are to be reproduced from the written symbols. Remind the students that what they read aloud should sound exactly like what they would *say.* Proper eye training is essential. The student must learn to see an entire sense-making group at a time rather than individual letters, words, or misgrouped words. The eye should stop only three or so times per line, and should not do any "retakes" or backtracking. Comprehension should be immediate, and the background of visual association drills (with cards) will be invaluable in providing a store of familiar groups.

A sense-making group is usually one of the following: (1) **a noun construct,** (2) **a verb unit,** (3) **a prepositional phrase.** The noun construct consists of a noun, its article, and accompanying adjective(s). The pronunciation drill cards (Fig. 15) representing nouns are units of this kind. The student has already had much practice in speaking of them. The verb unit is a verb alone, or a verb plus an adverb, or a negative verb. If the verb is very short, the following sense-making group may combine with it. A prepositional phrase may nearly always be uttered as a unit, and is sometimes combined with another prepositional phrase.

An example of poor grouping would be:

The little / boy is not / playing in the / garden.

If this is said aloud, the nonsensical effect of poor grouping is obvious. The correct grouping for reading as well as for speaking would be:

The little boy   **/ is not playing**   **/ in the garden.**
NOUN CONSTRUCT   VERB UNIT (*negative*)   PREPOSITIONAL PHRASE

In reading, it is possible that a student will pause in the wrong place because he is inspecting the spelling of a word, or simply because he misses the sense. The eye must capture an entire sense-making group at a time so that the mind may direct its utterance as a unit. The student should realize that when he encounters a noun, it is probably accompanied by an article and an adjective. He should survey enough words at a glance to assure inclusion of the entire associated group.

D. Rapid Silent Reading. Ultra-rapid reading, or "scanning," is a special skill to be acquired only after a student can read aloud with excellent pronunciation, speed, and fluency. Scanning is a means by which the reader gleans information by reading at a much faster speed than that of articulated speech. This skill demands an intimate knowledge of the language and its style and an ability to recognize and relate key words. For this reason scanning is an objective only for advanced students—especially those beginning literary studies.

(1) Résumé Method. Rapid-reading proficiency is the result of special training, and cannot be left to chance. When the time comes to assign longer reading passages for homework in late second-year or early third-year classes in high school, students must be told what technique to use. The readings assigned are at first rather short—perhaps only two or three pages—and are gradually increased in length.

Students are required to submit a written résumé of the *important* facts and ideas contained in the assigned pages. The résumé is strictly limited to one page (or so) in length. Tell the students how to go about this job. The reading is to be done entirely in the foreign language, and *never by translation.* Here are some suggested directions to the students:

1. Read the first paragraph rapidly in the foreign language to get a **general idea** of the setting, characters, and frame of reference. You will probably not get all the details, but you will at least have a general idea of where the action is taking place and what is going on.
2. Re-read the same paragraph rapidly. This time more **details** will fall into place on the framework you gained from the first reading.
3. Write down a **list** of the things you learned from these two readings.
4. Repeat steps (1), (2), and (3) for each of the other paragraphs in the assignment.
5. Using the notes you have made for each paragraph, write a concise one-page **summary** of the important facts and ideas contained in the entire assignment. This will involve a critical choice, for not everything can be mentioned.

CAUTION: Do not use any direct quotations from what you have read.

The requirement that the student write a résumé forces him to organize his ideas—or to come face to face with a realization that his information is very meager. The mental effort necessary in putting one's ideas on paper is an excellent way to ward off the complacent thought that may on occasion flicker across a student mind: "Sure, I know more or less what *that*'s all about." When the results must be put down on paper, the degree of *more*ness or *less*ness becomes starkly apparent.

The final résumé must be neat, well organized, and carefully presented. The purpose of the limitation of space is to force the student to select only the really important information for inclusion. He must develop a concept of the genuinely significant movement of thought and fit minor details into the main flow of ideas. The teacher's time for reading this material is also a consideration.

When advanced students are assigned long portions of stories, novels, plays, and other works, the résumé system is an effective way to monitor their performance. In class usually only spot checks can be made, but the résumé will reveal the student's thoroughness and comprehension quite vividly.

Students may be informed of the recommended reading time for each assignment. Begin with a generous allowance of time for the double reading of paragraphs; gradually reduce the time so that near the end of the course the time suggested to the students is normal rapid reading time for one reading only.

(2) **Testing.** Testing of scanning or rapid silent reading is accomplished by ordinary, timed comprehension tests. The object, after all, is to develop speed of comprehension. The speed must be greater than that of articulated speech.

A connected prose passage of the grammatical and vocabulary level of the students is reproduced and the page distributed face down. On a signal the students turn the page over and read the passage rapidly. On another signal the sheets must again be placed face down. Questions may be asked, or a résumé may be required.

If testing the comprehension is by questionnaire, the following possibilities exist:

1. The test is given **in the laboratory.** After the passage has been read, the sheets are collected. Students put on headphones. A tape bearing the test questions is broadcast, with pauses. During the pauses—

   a. The student records his answers on an individual blank tape (3″ reel); this is marked with his name (also spoken at the end of the test) and graded by a teacher or assistant.

   b. The student marks a multiple-choice answer sheet. Only *answers* are given on the paper—the questions are strictly oral. The foreign language is used for both questions and written answers.

  2. The test is given **in the classroom.** The teacher asks questions orally and students mark a multiple-choice answer sheet. This is all done in the foreign language.

Other variations may be worked out: e.g. the questions could be in writing, and the answers written out in full.

33. Writing. The beginning student should be able to write anything he can say. (Elementary school classes are exempted from this objective by many teachers.) Once a unit has been mastered orally, the teacher shows the students the way in which it is written. The student *reads* first, and is then, as part of his outside assignment, asked to learn how to *write* the unit. This he does by writing, comparing with the model, and making more attempts until he has mastered the writing of a sentence. He must be cautioned to include all accent and punctuation marks, to observe capitalization, and to make the special characters and ligatures correctly.

Dictation is practiced as part of the writing training. A tape is assigned in the laboratory. The student reproduces the material on the tape by writing it. He then compares what he has written with a master copy. If the material is taken from his textbook, he is told on what page to find it so that he may make his corrections. After that he tries again for improvement. In class the teacher gives short dictations for practice and occasionally to be handed in for grading or monitoring.

A. Controlled Composition. The foreign language must serve the student as a vehicle for ideas. First these ideas were expressed orally. Now the student is asked to express them in writing. A traditional method has been to control and standardize the student's work by giving the ideas in English. This merely made the student a prisoner of his native tongue. If he is to express himself directly in the foreign language, he must be aided to free himself from English rather than be shackled to it.

An idea is therefore presented in visual form. A pictorial array (Fig. 15) is placed before the students. Since they can express the idea aloud and have learned the spelling, they now write it. A simple idea, such as is represented by four pictures (*train, arrive, station, noon*), is displayed and the teacher indicates that it is to be written with no elaboration:

The train / arrives at the station / at noon.

If the teacher wants more detail he can say, "Express this idea, indicating colors." If the sketches show color the students might then write:

The *red* train arrives at the *white* station at noon.

Or the teacher may say, "Express this idea indicating size." Students write:

The *long* train arrives at the *small* station at noon.

If still more elaboration is wanted, both size and color are required:

The *long red* train arrives at the *small white* station at noon.

Adverbs are elicited by calling for "frequency" [the train *always* arrives] or "manner." Instructions are given in the foreign language (as soon as possible).

This method controls the composition so that the teacher may correct all papers in a standard manner; yet no English is used. The teacher is assured that the vocabulary is within the students' scope, because the same cards used for the introduction of pronunciation were used for teaching reading and then writing.

B. Semi-controlled Composition. A single picture containing several objects (designated by nouns already known to the students) or persons, and depicting a rather specific activity, is displayed. This contrasts with previous techniques where every card had only one picture—only one object or verb abstraction. Looking at this picture (an example is shown in Fig. 17), the student observes that he can name the persons and objects shown. His composition develops by his making and writing the most elementary statement he can about each and every object or person in the picture; then he makes one (later two) elaboration:

BASIC STATEMENT	ELABORATION
1. There are three people.	1. It's the Lopez family.
2. The man is tall.	2. His name is Mr. Lopez.
3. The woman is beautiful.	3. She is Mr. Lopez's wife.
4. The little boy is happy.	4. He is Pedro, Mr. and Mrs. Lopez's son.
5. They are all looking at an automobile.	5. They want to buy it.

As more elaboration is called for in later drills, much more can be invented by the imaginative student: the ages, occupations, interests, motives of the characters represented. There is additional factual material there, too, such as (in the original) colors of the car, background, and clothing; the location, and other specific data. This kind of picture can

Fig. 17: Picture for Semi-controlled Composition

be found in the advertising pages of almost any magazine, pasted on a sheet of cardboard, and used for composition drill.

Class time need not be taken up with this exercise. Most textbooks have photographs or drawings that can be assigned for a composition. The student can do this as homework, using the same technique. For reading practice some of the compositions may be read aloud in class. The other students may then ask questions about the situation described, and the "author" may attempt an answer.

C. Free Composition. Advanced students apply their skill by selecting their own topics (approved by the teacher) and developing their own ideas without the restrictions imposed by the foregoing methods. Only excellent students should be asked to do this, and then only after they have demonstrated great proficiency in the other techniques. Teachers may require an outline first.

D. Correction of Compositions: Correction Symbol Method. A teacher of my acquaintance used to correct written homework conscientiously, writing in all the omitted words, making all corrections in full, and using gallons of red ink. When students got their papers back they glanced at the bespangled documents, said (at most) "Oh yeah," and discarded them without a further thought. No learning took place on the part of the students as a result of the teacher's expenditure of effort and ink. For this reason it is suggested that the correction symbol method of correction be adopted.

Students are supplied with a list of correction symbols. These symbols suggest the most common types of errors, and the list provides a brief rule for the correction of each error.* Symbols such as the following are used because they readily indicate the grammatical principle involved: *pu* means punctuation, *sp* spelling, *om* omission, *wo* word order, and the like. The list is arranged alphabetically, and each symbol is followed by the rule and a reference to the complete explanation in the textbook.

The teacher will check each homework paper, underlining errors in red. A symbol indicating the type of error is placed in the margin for each red mark in the homework. If more than one error appears on a single line, slashes are used to separate the correction symbols. The purpose is to identify each error for the student, tell what kind of mistake it is, give a rule for correction, and require the student to apply all this information to rewrite the work correctly. A corrected sentence might look like this:

12. Le garçons apprendent le français bien. *ag / sp / wo*

The symbol *ag* means agreement (*le* should be plural like the noun it accompanies); *sp* means that the verb is spelled wrong; *wo* means that *bien* is in the wrong place (word order).

The following day when this student gets the paper back, he cannot say "Oh yeah!" and discard it, because part of his work is to make the necessary corrections. At home he will take a fresh sheet of paper, write the usual heading, the date of the original, and the word "Corrections." Then he examines each sentence marked in red, studies the type of error

* A short handbook for this purpose is available in French. It is the *French Handbook and Guide* by Edward M. Stack, New York: American Book Company, 1960.

and the remedy, starts his mental wheels grinding, and rewrites those sentences. For sentence 12 he produces this:

12. **Les** garçons **apprennent bien** le français.

After engaging actively in this learning process, the student clips the correction page on *top* of the original and submits this file to the teacher on the next class day together with his regular homework for that day. The teacher may accept the corrections, or may make further symbols on the correction sheet. Corrections of corrections of corrections make an imposing file, and usually this file represents real student learning and effort which was not possible when the teacher made the corrections *for* the student.

This method has long been used in English composition with success, and its application to foreign language composition is long overdue.

Tests and Measurements

TESTS not only gauge a student's progress and proficiency, but often serve to motivate the learner and to give unity to portions of the material being studied at different times. Tests are a kind of academic radar, sending useful indications back to the teaching center, allowing the teacher to re-orient his work to overcome weaknesses and difficulties. Tests should be fair (based entirely on material carefully covered in the class and laboratory), of average difficulty (hard enough to discriminate the excellent students from the mediocre ones), and devoid of questions of a petty or trivial nature. In language teaching, the aim is for every student to be able to express himself immediately, accurately, and with native pronunciation; and to understand the spoken language as uttered at normal speed by educated natives in informal conversation. Tests should be devised to probe just these abilities and skills, and if the instruction has been good, all well-motivated and normally intelligent students ought to be able to show their excellence on the test.

Tests should be constructed as practical applications of the foreign language. They should not be *about* the language (e.g. concerning a "rule" of grammar, an organized paradigm of a verb, etc.). It is desirable for the student to demonstrate that he can use a direct object pronoun, for example, but not so important that he can state a principle about its use couched in grammatical jargon.

The hearing phase of instruction is tested by an *aural comprehension test;* speaking is tested by an *oral examination;* and tests for reading and composition have already been suggested in the preceding chapter. This chapter will present the main testing procedures used in conjunction with the aural-oral approach. It will be noted that some of the traditional methods are used in testing reading and writing, and that the methods used for the aural and oral examinations are really adaptations of more traditional tests.

118

34. Aural Comprehension Testing. An aural comprehension test measures the extent to which a student understands the foreign language when it is spoken with normal native speed and pronunciation.

A. Materials. The student is supplied with (a) an answer booklet, (b) a response sheet—or, if machine grading is to be used, an IBM answer sheet, and a special IBM pencil.

The examiner is prepared to present the questions orally, either by playing a tape or by reading aloud. The use of tape is preferred. The examination may be broadcast centrally and heard by students in the booths of the laboratory, or may be broadcast to several classrooms at once over a central system. The latter arrangement enables students in very large courses to be given their examination simultaneously.

B. Types of Questions. There are three types of questions used: (a) the *simple question,* (b) the *completion type,* and (c) the *logical-inference type.*

(1) Simple Question. The student hears a simple question aloud. This question is followed by a 10-second pause, during which he selects *one* of three answers for that question from his answer booklet, and marks his response sheet (IBM or other) to indicate his choice. For example, his answer booklet may contain the following answers for question number 13:

> 13. (a) février
> (b) octobre
> (c) décembre

He hears the question, *Quel est le dixième mois de l'année?* (What is the tenth month of the year?). Since *deuxième* (second), *dixième* (tenth), and *douzième* (twelfth) all sound nearly alike, the student's discrimination of sounds as well as general understanding is tested. (The sounds are [døzjɛm], [dizjɛm] and [duzjɛm].) Since the answers include the second, tenth, and twelfth months, the student cannot eliminate any by logic; he must hear and understand to get the correct answer. If he decided (correctly) that answer (b) was correct, he would indicate his answer thus:

> 13. (a) (b) (c) (d)
> ‖ █ ‖ ‖

In Spanish an example of the simple question would be as follows:

18. (a) en el invierno
    (b) en el refrigerador
    (c) en el infierno

The student reads these answers *before* the question is heard: *¿Cuándo se hiela el agua?* (When does water freeze?) Then he marks his answer sheet for that question and reads the answers for the next question so as to be well prepared.

Most questions must begin with the foreign language equivalents of *what, where, when, how, who,* and *why.* Questions are so devised that the content is independent of all material except the qualities inherent in the question and answer—that is, no answer should be based on the contents of stories read, of class situations, or other locally pre-determined "facts." In addition, an effort is made to avoid making the question so simple that a single word caught by the student will be sufficient to allow a correct choice. Finally, the *wrong* answers are determined by deciding what incorrect construction the student might logically put upon the oral question, and then devising answers that would be correct for the misinterpretation. (The French example above demonstrates this.)

(2) **Completion Type.** The completion type question is presented as follows. An incomplete sentence is given orally in the foreign language; the intonation clearly indicates that there is more to come. The student selects the most logical completion of the statement he has heard from among the three choices given for that question in his answer booklet. For example:

36. (a) l'hôpital
    (b) un médicament
    (c) un médecin

The question on the examination tape is *Quand je suis malade je vais voir* . . . (When I am sick I go to see . . . the hospital, some medicine, a doctor).

In Spanish:

36. (a) la cuenta
    (b) el cuento
    (c) el salario

The statement given orally on the tape is *Antes de salir del restaurante, Juan paga* . . . (Before leaving the restaurant, John pays . . . the bill, the story, the salary).

The omitted portion must always be at the *end* of the incomplete statement, as blanks in other positions are unmanageable orally. The same considerations for the selection of questions and answers pertain here as for the question-type.

(3) **Logical-Inference Type.** The student hears a statement in the foreign language. From his answer booklet he selects the one answer that is most logically deduced from the facts expressed in the statement:

> 75. (a) Il avait froid.
> (b) Il avait faim.
> (c) Il avait chaud.

The statement for number 75 is heard: *Albert a ouvert la fenêtre du restaurant.* (Albert opened the window in the restaurant. (a) He was cold. (b) He was hungry. (c) He was warm.) If all the student understood was the word *restaurant,* he might pick answer *b.* The most logical reason for opening the window would be *c.* The construction of this type of question is very difficult, and the "logic" used must be carefully worked out if contestation of the answers is to be avoided. This type of question can, if well prepared, be a very revealing measure of comprehension.

An example in Spanish:

> 80. (a) Va a darla a su hermano.
> (b) No necesita novio.
> (c) Busca un café.

The statement for question number 80 is: *Ella tiene hambre.*

C. Composition of the Examination. The examination consists of 100 statements in the foreign language. About one-third of them are of the question type, one-third incomplete statements, and one-third logical-inference type. These oral questions are recorded (although they *could* be read from a script by the teacher at the examination). The number of the question is given in English, so that there will be no confusion about this important matter. The question is read at normal native speed with conversational pronunciation. Then there is a 10-second pause for marking the response sheet and reading the answers for the next question to be heard.

The vocabulary and grammatical knowledge of the student up to the time of the examination must be considered in composing questions, so as to keep within their limits. Questions should be self-sufficient; that is, the answer should not depend on any particular story, lecture, or reading matter. Finally, answers are so contrived that a student cannot guess the correct answer on the basis of his having heard a fairly obvious key-word in the oral question (as would be the case if he heard a reference to *restaurant* in the question, and the right answer was the only one (of three) pertaining to dining).

D. Procedure in Test Administration. The students are assembled and the materials (§ 34A above) distributed. At the announced time the tape is started. The tape begins with a verbatim reading of the instructions, just as printed on the students' answer booklets. Below is reproduced a typical format for the answer booklet:

FRENCH 1
AURAL COMPREHENSION TEST
November 7, 1962

Part I (Questions 1 through 36)

Question Portion

You will hear a series of questions in French. From this answer booklet select the one answer that best responds to the question, and indicate that answer on your printed response sheet opposite the number of the question.

Example 0. **Quelle est la capitale de la France?**

    (a) Paris
    (b) Berlin
    (c) Rome

You would darken space (a), opposite question number 0 on the response sheet:

0. (a) (b) (c) (d)

Do not mark the answer booklet in any way.
The test will now begin:

1.¹ (a) très bien   2.² (a) octobre
   (b) Robert   (b) février
   (c) Marie   (c) décembre

36.[3] (a) très bien, merci   STOP.
(b) Je suis allé au cinéma.
(c) J'irai à la plage.

Part II (Questions 37 through 65)

Completion Type

You will hear an incomplete sentence in French. From your answer booklet select the *one* answer that *best* completes the oral statement, and indicate that answer on your printed response sheet.

Example 00: **La capitale de la France est . . .**

(a) Berlin
(b) Paris
(c) Londres

You would darken space (b), opposite question number 00:

00. (a) (b) (c) (d)

The test will now continue:

37.[4] (a) Robert.
(b) Marie.
(c) Robert et Marie.

38.[5] (a) votre mère?
(b) la date de la bataille de Waterloo?
(c) cette belle jeune fille?

65.[6] (a) la concierge.
(b) l'addition.
(c) l'imperméable.

[1] SCRIPT: **1. Comment s'appelle cette étudiante?** (What's that co-ed's name?) The student must notice the pronunciation of the final [t] sound in *étudiante* to get the right answer.

[2] SCRIPT: **2. Quel est le dixième mois de l'année?** (What's the tenth month of the year?) Discussed in § 34B (1).

[3] SCRIPT: **36. Où allez-vous demain?** (Where are you going tomorrow?)

[4] SCRIPT: **37. Ces étudiants s'appellent . . .** (The names of these students are . . .)

[5] SCRIPT: **38. Voulez-vous faire la connaissance de . . .** (Would you like to meet . . . (a) your mother, (b) the date of the battle of Waterloo, (c) that beautiful girl?)

[6] SCRIPT: **65. Il va pleuvoir. Apportez-moi . . .** (It's going to rain. Bring me . . . (a) the concierge, (b) the bill, (c) the raincoat.)

Part III (Questions 66 through 100)

Logical-Inference Type

You will hear a statement in French. From your answer booklet select the one answer that is most logically deduced from the facts expressed in the oral statement, and indicate that answer on your printed response sheet.

Example 000: **Paris est la capitale de la France.**

  (a) Paris est une grande ville.
  (b) Paris est situé sur la Seine.
  (c) Paris est le siège du gouvernement.

You would select answer (c), and indicate that answer by darkening space (c) opposite question number 000 on your response sheet:

000. (a) (b) (c) (d)

The test will now continue.

66.[7] (a) Je suis riche.
  (b) Il est l'heure du dîner.
  (c) J'ai faim.

67.[8] (a) C'est le premier jour de la semaine.
  (b) Il faut aller à l'église.
  (c) C'était hier vendredi.

100.[9] (a) It's a long time between meals.
  (b) It's a standing date.
  (c) It's a kind of a mania.

STOP

In giving the oral questions, the question number is stated first *in English,* then the question (or statement) in the foreign language; then

[7] SCRIPT: **66. Je vais acheter le restaurant.** (I'm going to buy the restaurant. (a) I'm rich, (b) It's dinner time, (c) I'm hungry.)

[8] SCRIPT: **67. C'est aujourd'hui samedi.** (Today is Saturday. (a) It's the first day of the week, (b) One must go to church, (c) Yesterday was Friday.)

[9] SCRIPT: **100. Je dîne avec des amis le lundi.** (I always have dinner with some friends every Monday.) (Answers are sometimes given in English in the logical-inference part, since some of the inferences have to be couched in terms beyond the vocabulary range of the students. For more advanced students, all answers are in the foreign language.)

a pause is allowed long enough for the student to mark his answer, and to read the answers to the next question.

If IBM grading is to be used, standard IBM printed response sheets are provided; otherwise a mimeographed or spirit-duplicated response

No. ____________ NAME ________________________________

Examination Sheet No. ________ Last (PRINT) First MI

Be sure to enter this number, as examinations lacking this information will not be graded.

COURSE ______________ Section ________

DATE ________________________________

ANSWER SHEET

	A	B	C	D		A	B	C	D		A	B	C	D
1.	( )	( )	( )	( )	35.	( )	( )	( )	( )	68.	( )	( )	( )	( )
2.	( )	( )	( )	( )	36.	( )	( )	( )	( )	69.	( )	( )	( )	( )
3.	( )	( )	( )	( )	37.	( )	( )	( )	( )	70.	( )	( )	( )	( )
4.	( )	( )	( )	( )	38.	( )	( )	( )	( )	71.	( )	( )	( )	( )
5.	( )	( )	( )	( )	39.	( )	( )	( )	( )	72.	( )	( )	( )	( )
6.	( )	( )	( )	( )	40.	( )	( )	( )	( )	73.	( )	( )	( )	( )
7.	( )	( )	( )	( )	41.	( )	( )	( )	( )	74.	( )	( )	( )	( )
8.	( )	( )	( )	( )	42.	( )	( )	( )	( )	75.	( )	( )	( )	( )
9.	( )	( )	( )	( )	43.	( )	( )	( )	( )	76.	( )	( )	( )	( )
10.	( )	( )	( )	( )	44.	( )	( )	( )	( )	77.	( )	( )	( )	( )
11.	( )	( )	( )	( )	45.	( )	( )	( )	( )	78.	( )	( )	( )	( )
12.	( )	( )	( )	( )	46.	( )	( )	( )	( )	79.	( )	( )	( )	( )
13.	( )	( )	( )	( )	47.	( )	( )	( )	( )	80.	( )	( )	( )	( )
14.	( )	( )	( )	( )	48.	( )	( )	( )	( )	81.	( )	( )	( )	( )
15.	( )	( )	( )	( )	49.	( )	( )	( )	( )	82.	( )	( )	( )	( )
16.	( )	( )	( )	( )	50.	( )	( )	( )	( )	83.	( )	( )	( )	( )
17.	( )	( )	( )	( )	51.	( )	( )	( )	( )	84.	( )	( )	( )	( )
18.	( )	( )	( )	( )	52.	( )	( )	( )	( )	85.	( )	( )	( )	( )
19.	( )	( )	( )	( )	53.	( )	( )	( )	( )	86.	( )	( )	( )	( )
20.	( )	( )	( )	( )	54.	( )	( )	( )	( )	87.	( )	( )	( )	( )
21.	( )	( )	( )	( )	55.	( )	( )	( )	( )	88.	( )	( )	( )	( )
22.	( )	( )	( )	( )	56.	( )	( )	( )	( )	89.	( )	( )	( )	( )
23.	( )	( )	( )	( )	57.	( )	( )	( )	( )	90.	( )	( )	( )	( )
24.	( )	( )	( )	( )	58.	( )	( )	( )	( )	91.	( )	( )	( )	( )
25.	( )	( )	( )	( )	59.	( )	( )	( )	( )	92.	( )	( )	( )	( )
26.	( )	( )	( )	( )	60.	( )	( )	( )	( )	93.	( )	( )	( )	( )
27.	( )	( )	( )	( )	61.	( )	( )	( )	( )	94.	( )	( )	( )	( )
28.	( )	( )	( )	( )	62.	( )	( )	( )	( )	95.	( )	( )	( )	( )
29.	( )	( )	( )	( )	63.	( )	( )	( )	( )	96.	( )	( )	( )	( )
30.	( )	( )	( )	( )	64.	( )	( )	( )	( )	97.	( )	( )	( )	( )
31.	( )	( )	( )	( )	65.	( )	( )	( )	( )	98.	( )	( )	( )	( )
32.	( )	( )	( )	( )	66.	( )	( )	( )	( )	99.	( )	( )	( )	( )
33.	( )	( )	( )	( )	67.	( )	( )	( )	( )	100.	( )	( )	( )	( )
34.	( )	( )	( )	( )										

DO NOT WRITE BELOW: 100

No. Wrong ________ - ________

No. Right ________

Fig. 18: Response Sheet

sheet such as shown in Fig. 18 is produced locally. Such a sheet can be scored rapidly by making a perforated key. This is done by marking the correct answers on one sheet, and then cutting a hole at the location of these correct responses. By placing this key on top of a student sheet the teacher can quickly mark each hole where *no answer appears* on the student page. These are the wrong (or omitted) answers. If the student's mark can be seen through the hole in the key, his answer corresponds with the key and is correct.

The same form of aural comprehension test can be presented entirely in oral form. The student is furnished only a response sheet (and IBM pencil if appropriate). Both stimuli and responses are given orally on the tape. Now it is most important to keep the utterances very short; in the case of incomplete sentences (Part II), the complete sentence is repeated three times, one for each possible way:

> 41. (a) Cette étudiante s'appelle Robert.
> (b) Cette étudiante s'appelle le garçon.
> (c) Cette étudiante s'appelle Francine.

Here the incomplete statement consisted of *Cette étudiante s'appelle* (This co-ed's name is . . .), but the student does not have to bear this in mind while hearing three alternative answers. The first part (incomplete statement) is repeated with each possible completion (*Robert, le garçon, Francine*).

The totally oral presentation of such a test has several advantages. It sharpens the student's aural attention, reduces reliance on written representations, and saves much time in preparation of answer booklets. At the beginning stages of instruction, when emphasis is put rather fully on hearing and speaking, this mode of testing is preferable. It can, in fact, be profitably used at all stages and levels of instruction.

E. Scoring. Response sheets may be scored by hand or by machine. In both cases a key is used to facilitate the process. A score may be obtained by use of the formula

$$S = R - \frac{w}{2}$$

where S is the *score*, R is the number *right*, and *w* is the number *wrong*. The score is therefore the number of correct answers, minus half of the number of wrong answers. This formula compensates for the probability that the student will correctly *guess* one-third of the answers in a multiple-choice questionnaire of this kind.

An alternative is simply to use the number of correct answers as the student's score. While this is less scientific, the relative proficiency of students in aural comprehension is nonetheless indicated with good reliability. Often the scores are converted to letter grades by use of the "normal curve," regardless of the choice of scoring methods.

F. Practice Tapes. Students can gain needed practice in preparation for aural comprehension examinations (as well as for oral examinations) by use of practice tapes. In as much as the construction of aural comprehension tests is very difficult and time consuming, the teacher cannot hope to provide sample tests. Instead, an effective short cut is made by the device described below.

A master tape is made containing a series of questions, incomplete statements, and statements of the logical-inference type. The student uses this tape in the laboratory for practice, but he does not have an answer booklet. He takes a blank piece of paper and a pencil, and for each question jots down a *reasonable* short answer (just a word or two):

SOUND ON TAPE	STUDENT LISTENS AND WRITES:
Tape F1-507. Practice aural comprehension tape. Jot down a reasonable answer (just a word or two) for each question.	
Question type.	
1. What do you need to write on the blackboard? (*Pause*)	1. chalk
2. What do you wear when it rains? (*Pause*)	2. a raincoat
Logical-Inference Type.	
45. I'm tired. (*Pause*)	45. Go to bed.
46. I never study French. (*Pause*)	46. You'll flunk.
47. I bought a new car. (*Pause*)	47. Capitalist!
Incomplete Sentence Type	
73. When I have a headache, I take . . . (*Pause*)	73. an aspirin
74. Bob is going to the library to . . .	74. borrow a book.

When the series of questions is over, the answer portion enables the student to check his work. Now each question is repeated as given originally, the English translation given, and the original sentence again, followed by a pause for repetition. The student will know if his answer is sensible—any correct answer will do, provided the answer is specific enough to show comprehension.

The examples above are in English. On the practice tape, the foreign language would be used for all the sound on tape (except the English portion of the answers). If students have about ten to twenty such questions per week in the laboratory, they will be very well prepared for aural comprehension examinations by the end of the semester.

35. Oral Examinations. An oral examination measures the student's proficiency in expressing himself in the foreign language. His performance may be judged on (a) **immediacy** of response, (b) **excellence** of pronunciation, and (c) **appropriateness** (accuracy) of response.

An oral examination can be given individually by the teacher to each student in his office; or, if a library-type language laboratory is available, the examination may be administered to many students at a time. The availability of a laboratory having facilities for recording the performance of the students is assumed in this section, but the principles may be applied to other situations.

The general nature of the examination is this: the student hears a number of questions (let us say 12) broadcast to him as he sits at the laboratory booth. Pauses are allowed after each question, and the student answers the question in the foreign language. His answers (together with the questions*) are recorded. The recording is done on a small individual tape in the library-type laboratory, or at a centrally located recorder controlled by the teacher. The examination is short, for the teacher must later listen to all the answers and score them. So much can be said in two minutes, however, that an accurate judgment of a student's proficiency can be made in a tape of about that length.

A. Materials. Each student entering the library-type laboratory is supplied with a small reel of blank tape (a standard 3-inch reel in a box). Each tape and box is numbered for identification prior to issue to the students. No further materials are needed by the students.

The master tape for the examination (previously prepared by the teacher) consists of (a) instructions, (b) 10 to 20 pre-recorded questions, with appropriate pauses for student answers, and (c) closing instructions.

B. Types of Questions. An adequate test of a student's oral proficiency can be made in a very short time. Questions similar to those used in basic pronunciation drills and in class conversation are posed (e.g. How are you? What did you do last night? Where did you go Sunday? What's your Spanish teacher's name? When do you have lunch?). A period of 10 seconds silence is sufficient for an answer to this kind of question.

---

* New equipment will automatically record answers only in the laboratory, so that the teacher need not repeatedly hear the questions during grading.

C. Procedure and Format. Students take places in their booths, load the blank tape onto the machine, and set controls so as to receive the examination broadcast and simultaneously record their responses. If remote control of student tape movements is built into the laboratory, the teacher will start and stop all tapes in the laboratory. Otherwise students will start their own tapes when so instructed by the broadcast signal.

The first part of the examination master tape contains instructions. This portion is not recorded on the student tapes, since the teacher does not want to hear instructions every time he grades a tape. Student tapes are therefore motionless as the broadcast begins:

Oral examination, Spanish 1. Instructions. You will hear a series of questions in Spanish. After each question there will be a pause during which you should answer the question in Spanish. Adequate time is given for your response, but if you delay too long, you may miss the chance to answer. You will be judged upon the immediacy of your answer, the excellence of your pronunciation, and the appropriateness of the reply.

Now start your tapes to record your answers.

[*Brief pause for students to put tapes in motion. If remote controls are used, teacher starts tapes at this time, and this direction is omitted.*]

The test will now begin.

Number one: **¿Se levanta Vd. temprano?**
  Pause
Number two: **¿Cómo está Vd.?**
  Pause
Number three: **¿Habla español su padre?**
  Pause

Number twenty: **¿A dónde es necesario ir para comprar un libro?**
  Pause
  End of Spanish questions. Now answer in English: **What is your name?**
  Pause

Stop your tapes (*or teacher stops tapes by remote control*). Listen to the following directions.

As soon as you receive the signal, rewind your tapes onto the small reel, place the reel of tape in the box, and (give them to the teacher as you leave the room *or other appropriate instructions*). Do this now.

End of tape S1-505, Oral Examination, January 1961.

Such an oral examination assures absolutely standard and equitable conditions for all students being examined. All have the same time allowance, the same questions given in the same tone of voice and at the same speed. Such *is not* the case when students must go to the teacher's office one at a time, greet the teacher, indulge in small talk to relieve the tension, and combat interruptions such as telephone calls. Then too, the teacher cannot be sure the questions are exactly the same,

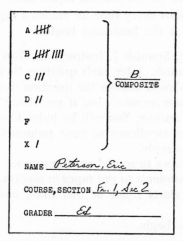

Fig 19: Oral Examination Scoring Slip

nor can he control and standardize many other factors involved in these personal interviews. In addition to eliminating inequities, the oral examination tape actually saves much time in administering and grading the examination.

D. Grading. The oral examination is graded with the aid of a simple mimeographed slip of paper (Fig. 19). The teacher puts the tape to be graded on a tape player and hears the first question and the student's response. Immediacy of response is the first criterion, so the teacher's pencil is poised opposite A to make a tick mark if the student answers (well) at once, but if there is a delay, the pencil point moves down opposite B, then C, etc. on the basis of immediacy.

When the student gives his response, the pencil may be opposite B (on the basis of some delay in answering). The teacher now considers the *excellence of pronunciation* and *appropriateness* of response. If both of these are excellent, a tick mark is made at B; if the pronunciation is

excellent, but the response is not appropriate (e.g. the answer is a beau-
tifully pronounced "Fine, thank you" to the question "Where are you
going?"), the tick mark is reduced to *D*.

Immediacy determines the *highest* grade the student can make on a
response; the other two factors may further reduce the grade on an
answer, but may not increase it above the immediacy ranking.

If a student fails to answer a question, he is given **x** on the scoring slip.
If the student is very poor in all respects, he is given *F*.

The tick marks will pile up on the scoring slip, so that after 12 questions
the tendency of a student to be excellent or miserable will be obvious.
Excellent students are rated *A*, failing ones, *F*. The rest are *C* students,
except that those *C* students tending toward excellence are given *B*, and
those tending toward mediocrity are given *D*.

The tape need not be stopped during scoring, for the tick marks are
made on the basis of rapid judgments using the three criteria mentioned.
At the end of the last question the student states his name; and this is
recorded at the bottom of the scoring slip. The grade is later transferred
to the teacher's grade book.

36. Dictation. Dictation is an excellent method of testing comprehension, grammatical knowledge, and spelling. It is normally used as a routine classroom procedure in the reading-writing phase of instruction in
each unit of work. It is used as a testing procedure of this phase of
instruction also. Dictation gives clear evidence (a) that the student can
spell what he hears, (b) that he hears accurately or inaccurately, (c)
that he is hearing everything, or that he is missing some important sounds,
(d) that he writes only things that make sense, or that he writes nonsense
and thereby demonstrates faulty understanding, (e) that he is aware
of subtleties of writing that do not appear in the oral form of the language,
such as past participle agreements and silent endings of verbs (**-ent** in
French), accent marks, punctuation, capitalization, and other features
difficult to test in any other closely controlled way.

37. Written Examinations. A written examination is used after the
student has mastered the aural and oral aspects of a certain portion of the
scheduled study. (Literary studies are excluded from this treatment.)
If the aural-oral presentation has been effective, the student will select
and spell his written answers on the basis of what he would normally say.

In selecting an answer to one of the questions such as those illustrated
in Fig. 20, the student will say the sentence in question to himself, and
determine the correct answer by the fact that it *sounds* right, rather than

132

RECOPY ALL ANSWERS HERE	

II. VERBS. <u>Supply the appropriate form of the verb whose infinitive is shown in parentheses.</u>

26._____ Hier je_____(aller) au cinéma avec Henri.

27._____ Je_____(se lever) à sept heures comme

28._____ d'habitude, et je_____(descendre) à la salle

29._____ à manger. Maman_____(être) dans la cuisine

30._____ où elle était en train de_____(préparer) mon

31._____ petit déjeuner. Quand elle me_____(voir),

32._____ elle_____(dire): Bonjour, petit. Comment

33._____ _____(aller) -tu ce matin?

****

III. PRONOUNS. <u>Supply the appropriate pronouns in the blanks provided.</u>

Mon professeur croit que mon ami Alain

51._____ n'est pas très intelligent._____a raison, le

52._____ professeur._____regarde Alain pour_____

53._____ poser une question facile. Alain a l'intention

54._____ de_____répondre, mais il ne réussit jamais

55._____ à_____faire.

****

IV. NOUN CONSTRUCTS: The PARTITIVE. <u>Supply either the partitive, general article, de, or other word needed. If nothing should be in blank, make an "x" there.</u>

En entrant dans le restaurant, Robert

76._____ pensait, -- Que j'aime_____rosbif! Je vais

77._____ commander_____rosbif,_____pommes de terre,

78._____ _____haricots,_____vin (beaucoup_____

79._____ vin, n'est-ce pas?), et comme dessert,_____

80._____ glace. . . . Le garçon a apporté l'addition.

81._____ Robert a cherché_____argent qu'il fallait

82._____ donner au garçon. Il a découvert qu'il n'avait

83._____ pas_____argent sur lui, mais il se souvenait

84._____ qu'il y avait_____argent sur la table dans sa

85._____ chambre, à la maison.

BE SURE THAT YOU HAVE COPIED ALL ANSWERS ACCURATELY INTO THE ANSWER COLUMN. IF ELISIONS WERE NECESSARY, THE EXACT SPELLING SHOULD BE COPIED, INCLUDING THE APOSTROPHE.

CHECK CAREFULLY BEFORE HANDING IN YOUR PAPER

Fig. 20: Extract from Written Examination

because of a "rule." This is just what a person does in his native language: he refers to *how he ordinarily says a thing* to determine usage.

Written examinations should confront the student with only such portions of the language as he has encountered previously in oral form. The problems should be those of practical application of the language—language in use, rather than such out-of-context things as lists of adjectives, or verb paradigms. It is in the field of testing that textbook exercises (objected to as often impractical for oral drills) might indeed be used. It is recommended that connected passages with fill-in blanks be used. Each passage is limited to blanks testing one kind of thing: one for verbs, one for noun constructs, one for pronouns, etc.

For ease of scoring, blanks are numbered. In the margin there are additional blanks bearing the same numbers. If the student is instructed to recopy his answers in these marginal blanks, a teacher's key can then be laid alongside the student's answers for rapid grading. If any question arises about the student's answer, the full passage is right at hand.

A. Comprehension of Reading. Reading comprehension may be tested by having on the examination paper a series of short prose paragraphs. The student reads the paragraphs, and then may (a) answer questions printed under each paragraph, using full responses, or (b) select one of several statements under each, choosing the one statement most logically deduced from the facts expressed in the paragraph. The latter is much like the logical-inference questions of the aural comprehension examination, except that in the reading test there is much more material to consider before drawing a logical conclusion. The second method (b) is used for rapid scoring.

B. Translation. Translation to or from English is not used on the elementary or intermediate levels usually, because the purpose of instruction is to establish the foreign language as an independent mode of communication.

Controlled composition will serve the purpose of discovering whether the student can write the foreign language. The control on an examination may be a picture like that in Fig. 17 (§ 33B), either reproduced on the examination paper or enlarged to be displayed to all examinees at once.

Questionnaires may be used to elicit compositions that are as good as translations for evaluating the student's writing ability. Idioms like *avoir faim* (to be hungry) can be evoked by such questions as "Why do you go to the restaurant?" in the foreign language.

Multiple-choice selections may be used for testing the knowledge of word-order, spelling, agreements, and so on. A statement is made in the foreign language, and it is followed by several choices of a second sentence that logically follows the first. For example:

> 18. Voilà nos professeurs.
>   (a) Ils parle français bien.
>   (b) Il parle bien le français.
>   (c) Ils parlent bien le français.
>   (d) Ils parlent le français bien.

Translation from English to the foreign language, and vice versa, is an art reserved for advanced students. If the examination for beginning students must require strictly controlled composition for the sake of making the grading standard, that composition should be controlled by pictures (as in basic oral drills), or by replies elicited in the manner of oral drills for the laboratory. The main use of English in examinations seems to be simply to get all students to say exactly the same thing; this result can be achieved without the use of English.

Exercises

I

The Force of Language

Chapter 1, pages 3-6

1. Animals can analyze and predict the future without use of language; for example, dogs know when to return home for meals, rats can solve mazes; even insects have complex social organization, as do ants. Bearing this in mind, write a short analytic comparison between man's abilities and those of other animals. What limitations are imposed on animals with respect to analysis, prediction, and solving of problems? Does *language* free man of these limitations? How? To what extent?

2. Define *culture*. Write a brief sketch of a cultureless (imaginary) human society, and then analyze what life in such a society would be like as compared with life in a rich culture. Then show what part language would play in each of these societies.

3. Give an impressive example of hostility that has arisen because of ignorance. What part did language play in the instance you have cited? What part did culture play? How was the situation finally resolved?

4. What are the objectives of language teaching? How can the objectives be attained?

5. Consider the value of learning a second language as thoroughly as the native language. Propose some strong arguments *against* learning a second language. Refute these arguments.

6. Delineate and explain the proper sequence of teaching a foreign language using the aural-oral method. What methods could be used for each step?

II

Construction of Aural–Oral Drills

Chapter II, pages 7-31

1. Examine a beginning language textbook to determine whether the drills and exercises are suitable for immediate use as aural-oral drills. Select one that is *not* suitable, state the reasons, and rewrite the drill in patterned form suitable for reading onto a master tape.

2. What three general principles apply to oral drills? Can you add some other principles to the list? Do so.

3. In Section 1 of this chapter (*adjectives*), there are many examples given. You will notice that the example numbers often are not consecutive. This means that a part of the pattern is missing. For example, in the very first group in French, the numbers are 41, 42, 43, and 50.

Select any set of examples in this section, and continue any sequence that is started but not finished. In the example just mentioned, you would write pairs for number 44 through 49, following a pattern. Select enough different parts so that you will have written at least 12 pairs (stimulus-response pairs) for this exercise.

4. Continue one of the open-end mutation drills in Section 3 wherever it is interrupted in the text, so that at least eight pairs of any pattern are created by your contribution.

5. Make a list of six regular verbs of one conjugation in the language of your choice. Prepare a pattern drill to teach the present-tense forms of these verbs in the *you* and *I* forms only (second personal plural and first person singular).

III

Types and Patterns of Oral Drills

Chapter III, pages 32-47

1. Describe fully the teaching phase and the testing phase of an oral drill. Select a grammatical point (structural or inflexional) and analyze it for drill construction purposes. Show your analysis in tabular form, like those in the text. State the probable length of the drill in minutes. Indicate the best type of pattern for teaching the point, and write the first 15 pairs in script form (refer to Fig. 11, page 79). Subdivide if necessary to keep the total drill down to 14 minutes. Use anticipation mode.

2. Open an elementary grammar book to about the middle of the book. Examine the exercises used to teach the grammatical content of the lesson. Give a detailed criticism of each major exercise in the lesson, dealing specifically with patterning of the material, types of drills, adaptability to recording for oral drills.

If you find one that is unsatisfactory, rewrite it, using the same grammatical principle being taught and the vocabulary to that point. Use standard format and present your script in full, ready to be read by another speaker in the recording studio.

3. Open an elementary text at random, and take the next exercises in the book at the point you open it. Decide what pattern would be best for oral drills on each of the exercises. Write five pairs as a sample of each type, based on the exercises you have selected. State (a) the

nature of the grammatical point, (b) the oral drill type, and (c) your pairs in script form.

IV

The Language Laboratory

Chapter IV, pages 48-58

1. Define in your own words what is meant by a broadcasting-type laboratory as contrasted with a library-type. State the circumstances under which it would be more advantageous to use one rather than the other.

2. A kind of laboratory called a "listening laboratory" exists. The student simply listens but does not talk. What criticisms can be leveled at this kind of laboratory from the teaching point of view?

3. Some educators advocate laboratories in which there is "instantaneous hearing" but no recording. It is claimed that if the student hears himself electronically at the same moment he speaks, that is sufficient for the self-critical process. Yet often one hears a conversation like this:

A. I have some stastistics to prove it.
B. You mean *statistics?*
A. That's what I *said.*

This kind of exchange seems to indicate that a person does *not* hear himself critically enough as he speaks, and that a recording (with comparison features) would give him a more objective basis for self-criticism and improvement linguistically.

State your own views about this, and support them with cogent arguments. (If assigned, prove experimentally in a laboratory.)

4. Select an actual room in your institution. Measure it; draw a floor plan showing dimensions. Then select laboratory equipment from available catalogues. Using actual dimensions plot the position of all booths, rooms, cabinets, racks, doors and windows, console, and other components of the laboratory. Write a well-organized description of this laboratory, including all specifications of construction and installation.

5. Criticize your plans and specifications (above) on the basis of needs for a language enrollment of 435 students distributed into French, German, and Spanish in about equal proportions. Assume that the installation is for a high school, that there are six 40-minute periods per day, that the largest elementary class in any language has 38 students. If you make any other assumptions necessary for your criticism, state them at the outset.

V

Tape Library and Student Routine

Chapter V, pages 59-71

1. Using any elementary textbook, assume that the course number is 1, that you have already made 34 master tapes in the course, and that you are about to make another. Open the textbook three-fourths of the way through; using that lesson, assign the next tape number to it. Now prepare on 3 x 5 cards the necessary cards for the card catalogue. Include such cross-reference cards as are desirable.

2. Compute the number of student tapes needed on the shelves for French 3 under the library system, comparing the situation using *tape retirement* and that using *full strength* of tapes for all lessons. Assume that there are usually 12 tapes on the shelf for the current lesson for that course, and that there are 25 lessons projected for the semester. If a full 5-inch reel of Mylar tape costs the school $1.50, how much money in student tapes (half-reels) is tied up on the shelf under each system?

3. Inspect the language laboratory most convenient to you. Write an orientation tapescript to be used in teaching new students to use the equipment and the laboratory in general. Base your script on the actual equipment and layout of the laboratory.

4. Investigate sources of commercially pre-recorded tapes for use in an elementary course. Report the best sources and indicate generally to what extent the tapes correlate with specific textbooks. What can be done with taped elementary material that is not geared to a specific text you are using to teach from?

VI

Laboratory Administration

Chapter VI, pages 72-83

1. Draw up a formal proposal for your chief administrative official, outlining the personnel (and their specific duties) needed for the operation of a language laboratory in your school. Adapt the general principles given in this chapter to your particular institution (either where you actually teach, or a school whose situation you know well).

2. Prepare simple instructions to be duplicated and circulated to all language teachers in your school. These instructions are to inform them of (a) the facilities of the laboratory in general, (b) the advantage of using it, (c) the manner in which they and their students will be sched-

uled for its use, (d) exactly what their responsibility is in the laboratory, (e) what administrative routine is required of them, and (f) how they go about making tapes, and arranging for their students to hear them.

All this is specifically oriented toward an actual school situation with which you are familiar.

3. Prepare a requisition to the supply department, listing all small pieces of equipment, tools, stationery and office supplies, etc. that you will need in your laboratory. Include some items not mentioned in the text.

VII

Classroom Procedures

Chapter VII, pages 84-104

1. Make a class lesson plan for a lesson (or unit) in an elementary text of your choice. Include post- and pre-laboratory work, and indicate quite specifically what will be done with the balance of a 40-minute class period.

2. Assuming that the rest of your methods class knows something about the language you are teaching, and that they are your elementary students, present a new sound for hearing and speaking. State at the outset what you assume they *have* had among the sounds in the word(s) you will use in your presentation. Use critical hearing drills, then pronunciation practice with physiological clues.

For this drill select a sound of the foreign language that is difficult— i.e. one not exactly the same as an English sound.

3. Prepare an array of pronunciation drill cards, using a basic sentence of four cards and three patterned changes. (You will need to make seven cards—more if you wish.) Drill the class on sentence structure and intonation, using native conversational speed. Assume that they have already learned to pronounce all the sounds and words represented by your cards.

4. Invent and concisely state (in writing) a situation drill that could be done in class after your students had gone halfway through an elementary text of your choice.

Write out the dialogue you would expect as a result of the situation you have proposed.

5. Write a description of a simple game that could be played (a) in elementary school classes of the fifth-grade level, *or* (b) in high school classes at the beginning language level. Make the description clear, so that if it were given to the students, orally or in writing, they would know how to play.

State the advantages and disadvantages of the game you have described, with special reference to the contribution it makes to language teaching.

6. If the institution you are now in has an audio-visual center or library, find out and report in writing what films and filmstrips are immediately available in the elementary course in the language of your choice. Preview *one* film or filmstrip of this kind, and give the class a critical analysis.

7. Select a short filmstrip of cultural value, and prepare an anticipation drill (one four-phase sequence for each frame of the filmstrip). Write out the entire tapescript for the filmstrip. Present the filmstrip and accompanying drill in class.

VIII

Reading and Writing Objectives

Chapter VIII, pages 105-17

1. Prepare a drill designed to teach students consistent spellings in the foreign language you have selected. For example, the sound [u] is always spelled *ou* in French, and [y] is always spelled *u*. A dictation list of paired words like "la r*ou*te, la l*u*ne" would help drive this point home. Select a similar feature and make a dictation of at least five pairs; then select another feature and prepare a second dictation of five pairs.

2. If your main language is French, devise a dictation drill designed to teach students to write the silent plural verb ending **-ent** when it is needed.

3. If there are several letter combinations that are pronounced alike (as in French: *au, aux, eau; et, ez, é; ais, ait*), devise a drill for dictation using words containing these combinations.

4. Prepare a built-up drill for teaching reading in the laboratory, based on simple arrays of pictures. Sketch the first few of the pictures you have in mind for the drill.

5. Copy a passage of about twelve lines in the foreign language. Divide the passage into sense-making groups for reading onto tape as a coaching drill in reading skill. Make the tape.

6. Read about six pages in the foreign language rapidly. Time yourself. Write a résumé of the pages read, limiting the résumé to one page. Then make a simple list of the points you consider essential for a student to include in a résumé of this selection.

This preliminary work having been done, write an assignment to be given to your class. Tell them the pages to be read, the method of procedure for reading, the way in which a résumé should be prepared, and the time you would recommend (for them as beginners in rapid reading).

7. Prepare a laboratory comprehension examination for the same passage you read for question 6. The examination must be in script form; however, indicate the precise answer expected of the student.

8. Require the composition of five elaborated sentences, based upon five arrays of cards. The drill should be based upon vocabulary of the first half of the textbook being used. Write the five sentences expected. In class, display the arrays one at a time, and let the members of your class write their versions. Compare your sentences with those of the students to determine how closely controlled the exercise is.

9. Select a magazine advertisement for use in semi-controlled composition. Using oral techniques, elicit simple statements and elaborations from various members of the class. Then help organize the statements into a logical sequence. Require that the students then reproduce the oral composition in writing, from memory.

10. Determine what mistakes are most commonly made by students in writing the language of your specialty, and make a list of correction symbols to represent these errors.

Write a short composition demonstrating the errors and the use of your correction symbols.

IX

Tests and Measurements

Chapter IX, pages 118-34

1. Prepare a partial aural comprehension examination for the end of the first semester of work. Ten questions for each of the three main types of questions (a total of 30) will suffice. Write the examination in full: prepare a dummy answer booklet, complete with heading and instructions; and prepare the tapescript in good form.

2. Duplicate enough copies of your answer booklet for all members of your class. Make the master examination tape in the laboratory. Administer the examination to the members of your class in methods, and receive criticism gracefully.

3. Score the examinations administered in question 2, and announce the results in the form of letter grades. Explain to the class your method for arriving at the results.

4. Prepare a practice tape for aural comprehension containing 30 stimuli. Indicate on your script the response(s) expected for each stimulus, based on the vocabulary of the students at that moment.

5. Prepare a script for an oral examination of 20 questions. If a demon-

stration class of actual beginning students is available, base the examination on their state of training. Administer the examination to several students and grade the results.

Play some of the student response tapes in methods class so that all may have a chance to use the scoring slips. See to what extent they agree on the grade for the examinee.

6. Prepare a written examination passage similar to one of those in Fig. 20. Confine the passage to one kind of grammatical principle. Have at least 20 blanks to fill in.

7. Prepare five short passages of about eight to ten typewritten lines each in the foreign language for use in testing reading comprehension. You may take passages from any source, and edit as you wish. Compose the passages into a valid test of reading comprehension, using questions or multiple-choice logical inferences.

Bibliographical Note

THE FOLLOWING PUBLICATION is a most complete listing of books, films, *realia*, services, and sources of supply. Its existence makes an exhaustive bibliography unnecessary here, and it is recommended that every teacher and prospective teacher of languages have a copy for reference:

> *Materials List for Teachers of Modern Foreign Languages*, Ed. Douglas W. Alden, New York: Modern Language Association, 1959, 85 pp. Price 50 cents.
>> *Obtainable from* MLA, *70 Fifth Avenue, New York 11, New York.*

TEACHERS should also read regularly and carefully the following journals to keep abreast of new techniques:

> *The French Review* (American Association of Teachers of French), Ed. Julian Harris, University of Wisconsin.
> *Hispania* (American Association of Teachers of Spanish and Portuguese), Ed. Robert G. Mead, Jr., University of Connecticut.
> *Modern Language Journal*, Ed. J. Alan Pfeffer, University of Buffalo.

THE FOLLOWING BIBLIOGRAPHY is available in most libraries, and is a useful source in locating articles and books on language teaching:

> Coleman, Algernon, *An Analytic Bibliography of Modern Language Teaching*, New York: King's Crown Press, 1949 (Vol. III).

FOR RECORDS, FILMS, AND FILMSTRIPS, the following books serve as primary sources of information:

> *French Records, A Catalogue.* New York: Cultural Services of the French Embassy (972 Fifth Avenue, New York 21, N. Y.).
> *Educational Film Guide.* New York: H. W. Wilson Co.
> *Filmstrip Guide.* New York: H. W. Wilson Co.

FOR THOSE TEACHING FRENCH, the following study is particularly important in selection of vocabulary:

> Gougenheim, G., Rivenc, P., Michéa, R., and Sauvageot, A., *L'Élaboration du français élémentaire*, Paris: Didier, 1956.

143

Use the Table of Contents for locating drills (by part of speech, structural function, and general topic) and main subjects.